Actionable Insights with Amazon QuickSight

Develop stunning data visualizations and machine learning-driven insights with Amazon QuickSight

Manos Samatas

BIRMINGHAM—MUMBAI

Actionable Insights with Amazon QuickSight

Publishing Product Manager: Sunith Shetty

Senior Editor: David Sugarman

Content Development Editor: Joseph Sunil

Technical Editor: Rahul Limbachiya

Copy Editor: Safis Editing

Project Coordinator: Aparna Nair

Proofreader: Safis Editing

Indexer: Sejal Dsilva

Production Designer: Roshan Kawale

First published: January 2022
Production reference: 2250122

Published by Packt Publishing Ltd.
Livery Place
35 Livery Street
Birmingham
B3 2PB, UK.

ISBN 978-1-80107-929-7

www.packt.com

To Gabriela

For her unconditional support and encouragement.

Contributors

About the author

Manos Samatas is a solutions architect specializing in big data and analytics. He has several years of experience developing and designing big data applications for various industries, including telecommunications, cybersecurity, healthcare, and the public sector. He is an accredited AWS **Subject Matter Expert** (**SME**) in analytics and he possesses the AWS Data Analytics Specialty and the AWS Solutions Architect Professional certifications. Manos lives in London with his fiancée Gabriela. In his free time, he enjoys traveling, socializing with friends, and taking care of his plants.

About the reviewers

Madhavan Sriram is a manager of data science at Amazon and focuses on building data-intensive products for Amazon's transportation business. His team processes over 200 TB of data annually to build intelligent products that enable automated warehouse operations by leveraging machine learning, big data, and visualisation techniques. His research focus areas are in the space of big data and machine learning from an applied context. In the past, he worked for several large enterprises including IBM, Toyota, and Royal Philips on furthering their science and data landscape. He and his wife reside in Luxembourg and enjoy spending the time outdoors with their furry golden retriever "Richard Parker".

Raquel Marasigan is an information security engineer II lead at CBSPI, where she analyses the effectiveness of security strategies. Raquel earned her Bachelor of Arts from Arellano University, majoring in political science. Her interest in technology and security motivated her to continue her education in data analytics. She is currently enrolled with the University of Asia and the Pacific, completing a Masters Applied Business Analytics degree, and completing her capstone project for the 2022 school year. Raquel is fortunate to work alongside the author, Jason Dunn, Mia Heard, and other experts in the AWS Community Builders and AWS Users Group where they share their insights. Many thanks to Raquel's two sons for their encouragement throughout the process of reviewing this book.

Table of Contents

3

Preparing Data with Amazon QuickSight

4

Developing Visuals and Dashboards

Section 2: Advanced Dashboarding and Insights

5
Building Interactive Dashboards

6
Working with ML Capabilities and Insights

7
Understanding Embedded Analytics

Section 3: Advanced Topics and Management

8
Understanding the QuickSight API

9
Managing QuickSight Permissions and Usage

10
Multitenancy in Amazon QuickSight

Other Books You May Enjoy

Index

Preface

The adoption of cloud-native **business intelligence** (**BI**) tools, such as Amazon QuickSight, enables organizations to gather insights from data at scale. This book is a practical guide to performing simple-to-advanced tasks with Amazon QuickSight.

You'll begin by learning QuickSight's fundamental concepts and how to configure data sources. Next, you'll be introduced to the main analysis-building functionality of QuickSight to develop visuals and dashboards. The book will also demonstrate how to develop and share interactive dashboards with parameters and onscreen controls. Advanced filtering options with URL actions will then be covered, before learning how to set up alerts and scheduled reports. Later, you'll explore the insight visual type in QuickSight using both existing insights and by building custom insights. Further chapters will show you how to add machine learning insights such as forecasting capabilities, analyzing time series data, adding narratives, and outlier detection to your dashboards. You'll also explore patterns to automate operations and look closer into the API actions that allow us to control settings. Finally, you'll learn about advanced topics such as embedded dashboards and multitenancy.

By the end of this book, you'll be well versed in QuickSight's BI and analytics functionalities that will help you create BI apps with ML capabilities.

Who this book is for

This book is for BI developers and data analysts who are looking to create interactive dashboards using data from modern data architecture on AWS with Amazon QuickSight. This book will also be useful for anyone who wants to learn Amazon QuickSight in depth using practical examples. You will need to be familiar with general data visualization concepts; however, no prior experience with Amazon QuickSight is required.

What this book covers

Chapter 1, Introducing the AWS Analytics Ecosystem, starts by introducing the AWS analytics ecosystem. Then we will discuss how Amazon QuickSight fits within the wider ecosystem. We will look closer at the modern data architecture and its benefits and different components. Finally, we will provide a step-by-step guide for the reader to set up this architecture in their development environment and add demo data that we will use with Amazon QuickSight to create visualizations later in the book.

Chapter 2, Introduction to Amazon QuickSight, introduces Amazon QuickSight and its main benefits as a cloud-native BI tool. We will explain the various options at the account creation stage, including the user authorization options. Finally, we will provide a step-by-step guide for the reader to set up a QuickSight account and configure the required permissions to connect to Amazon Redshift.

Chapter 3, Preparing Data with Amazon QuickSight, focuses on how to create data sources with Amazon QuickSight and use the dataset editor. We will provide a step-by-step guide to help readers set up data sources on their environment. Finally, we will look at more advanced operations such as joins, row-level security controls, and calculated fields.

Chapter 4, Developing Visuals and Dashboards, introduces the main analysis-building functionality of Amazon QuickSight. We will start by exploring the author UI and explain the different visual types. After adding certain visual types and explaining their functionality we will introduce the concepts of dashboards and stories and explain how we can share these dashboards with other users. Finally, we will look how to style a dashboard and create custom themes.

Chapter 5, Building Interactive Dashboards, explores how to develop interactive dashboards with Amazon QuickSight. The reader will learn to add custom controls on their dashboards and add interactivity to their BI application using parameters. We will also look at advanced filtering options with point-and-click actions with URL actions. Finally, we will explore the reader user experience via the web and mobile QuickSight app and we will explain how to set up alerts and scheduled reports.

Chapter 6, Working with ML Capabilities and Insights, explores the insight visual type in Amazon QuickSight. We will use both the QuickSight-suggested insights and build our own custom insights. We will add forecasting capabilities by analyzing time-series data, and we will add narratives and outlier detection. Finally, we will look more closely at how to integrate Amazon QuickSight with models deployed with Amazon SageMaker.

Chapter 7, Understanding Embedded Analytics, dives deeper into embedded dashboards. We will describe the architecture and the business drivers behind embedding, and we will explain the permission models. We will have a step-by-step guide to set up embedded analytics for authenticated or unauthenticated users. Finally, we will look briefly at how to embed the QuickSight console for QuickSight authors.

Chapter 8, Understanding the QuickSight API, explores patterns to automate certain operations using the QuickSight API. We will see how to create dashboards and reuse analyses using the Template API. We will also explore patterns to automate monitoring of dataset operations and finally, we will look more closely into the API actions that allow us to control settings.

Chapter 9, Managing QuickSight Permissions and Usage, focuses on data permissions and managing Amazon QuickSight operations. We will explain how it integrates with Lake Formation Redshift and Redshift Spectrum tables from a data authorization point of view. We will look at incident reporting using AWS CloudTrail and will examine the use of common operations to manage QuickSight usage.

Chapter 10, Multitenancy in Amazon QuickSight, talks about multitenancy in Amazon QuickSight. To understand it better, we will look at a simple hands-on example. Finally, we will look at an architecture that combines the two concepts of embedded analytics and multitenancy and explain its practical use cases.

To get the most out of this book

You will need to be familiar with general data visualization concepts, but won't need any previous experience with Amazon QuickSight. Also, we expect you to have a basic understanding of the AWS cloud.

If you are using the digital version of this book, we advise you to type the code yourself or access the code from the book's GitHub repository (a link is available in the next section). Doing so will help you avoid any potential errors related to the copying and pasting of code.

Please ensure that you terminate all running instances of AWS when not needed, to reduce costs.

Download the example code files

You can download the example code files for this book from GitHub at `https://github.com/PacktPublishing/Actionable-Insights-with-Amazon-QuickSight`. If there's an update to the code, it will be updated in the GitHub repository.

We also have other code bundles from our rich catalog of books and videos available at `https://github.com/PacktPublishing/`. Check them out!

Download the color images

We also provide a PDF file that has color images of the screenshots and diagrams used in this book. You can download it here: `http://www.packtpub.com/sites/default/files/downloads/9781801079297_ColorImages.pdf`.

Conventions used

There are a number of text conventions used throughout this book.

`Code in text`: Indicates code words in text, database table names, folder names, filenames, file extensions, pathnames, dummy URLs, user input, and Twitter handles. Here is an example: "For example, in QuickSight, the `DeleteDataSet` action deletes a dataset."

A block of code is set as follows:

```
$aws quicksight update-user --user-name author-iam  --role
AUTHOR --custom-permissions-name custom-author --email <your-
email> --aws-account-id <account-id> --namespace default
--region us-east-1
```

When we wish to draw your attention to a particular part of a code block, the relevant lines or items are set in bold:

```
{
    "Status": 200,
    "EmbedUrl": "https://us-east-1.quicksight.aws.amazon.
com/... ?code=...&identityprovider=quicksight&isauthcode=true",
    "RequestId": "21d2ad96-3c2b-42a4-ae10-8eb28b20892c"
}
```

Bold: Indicates a new term, an important word, or words that you see onscreen. For instance, words in menus or dialog boxes appear in **bold**. Here is an example: "With the **Manage Users** option selected, click on **Manage Permissions** as shown."

> **Tips or important notes**
> Appear like this.

Get in touch

Feedback from our readers is always welcome.

General feedback: If you have questions about any aspect of this book, email us at customercare@packtpub.com and mention the book title in the subject of your message.

Errata: Although we have taken every care to ensure the accuracy of our content, mistakes do happen. If you have found a mistake in this book, we would be grateful if you would report this to us. Please visit www.packtpub.com/support/errata and fill in the form.

Piracy: If you come across any illegal copies of our works in any form on the internet, we would be grateful if you would provide us with the location address or website name. Please contact us at copyright@packt.com with a link to the material.

If you are interested in becoming an author: If there is a topic that you have expertise in and you are interested in either writing or contributing to a book, please visit authors.packtpub.com.

Share Your Thoughts

Once you've read *Actionable Insights with Amazon QuickSight*, we'd love to hear your thoughts! Scan the QR code below to go straight to the Amazon review page for this book and share your feedback.

https://packt.link/r/1-801-07929-3

Your review is important to us and the tech community and will help us make sure we're delivering excellent quality content.

Section 1: Introduction to Amazon QuickSight and the AWS Analytics Ecosystem

This section is an introduction to Amazon QuickSight and modern data architecture. After completing this part, the reader will understand how to set up Amazon QuickSight, manage data sources, and build and share basic dashboards.

This section consists of the following chapters:

- *Chapter 1, Introducing the AWS Analytics Ecosystem*
- *Chapter 2, Introduction to Amazon QuickSight*
- *Chapter 3, Preparing Data with Amazon QuickSight*
- *Chapter 4, Developing Visuals and Dashboards*

1

Introducing the AWS Analytics Ecosystem

As data increases in both volume and variety, organizations from all verticals are adopting cloud analytics services for their data analytics. AWS offers a number of analytics services covering data lakes, data warehousing, big data processing, **extract, transform, load** (**ETL**), and data visualization. In this chapter, we will introduce the AWS analytics ecosystem. Some of the services we discuss here will be mentioned again later in the book.

First, we will map the AWS services into categories. Then, we will discuss how Amazon QuickSight fits into the wider AWS analytics ecosystem. We will look more closely at a modern modern data architecture and we will discuss its benefits and its components. Finally, we will provide a step-by-step guide to set up a data modern data architecture on AWS and load and query a demo data sample. Some of this information may already be familiar to you, but let's go back over the basics.

In this chapter, we will cover the following topics:

- Discovering the AWS analytics ecosystem
- Exploring the data modern data architecture on AWS
- Creating a basic modern data architecture

Technical requirements

To follow along with this chapter, you will need the following pre-requisites:

- An AWS account with console access
- AWS CLI access

The code sample for this chapter can be accessed on the GitHub repository for this book at `https://github.com/PacktPublishing/Actionable-Insights-with-Amazon-QuickSight/tree/main/chapter_1`.

Discovering the AWS analytics ecosystem

AWS provides a large number of analytics services. In addition to that, AWS has a number of partners who specialize in data analytics and offer analytics solutions that run on the AWS infrastructure. Partner solutions are not in the scope of this section, however. This section focuses on the AWS fully managed analytics services. In order to list the services, we will first define the specific categories related to analytics functions. Machine learning and predictive analytics are also out of the scope of this chapter. For every service category, we will then list the AWS services available, and for each service, we will provide a high-level description. *Figure 1.1* depicts the commonly used AWS analytics services.

Figure 1.1 – AWS analytics services

Business intelligence

More and more organizations aspire to be data-driven and use data to drive their strategic decisions. **Business intelligence** (**BI**) tools help organizations to transform data into actionable insights. With the use of BI tools, users can analyze data and then present their findings in reports or dashboards. These reports or dashboards can then be consumed by business users who are interested in getting a picture of the state of the business.

In 2015, AWS launched **Amazon QuickSight**, a cloud-native BI tool. Since then, AWS has added new features to QuickSight, enriching the standard dashboard functionality with machine learning capabilities and offering embedded dashboard functionality. Amazon QuickSight is the main technology we will be covering in this book. Over the next few chapters, we will start with the basic functionality of Amazon QuickSight, and then we will explore more advanced features. Where possible, we will use practical examples that can be repeated in your own development environment, to give you hands-on experience with Amazon QuickSight.

Data warehousing

Data warehouses are repositories of data; they are important components of the BI process. Data stored in data warehouses is typically structured. Traditionally, data is ingested and centralized into data warehouses from different operational data stores. Data warehouses are optimized to run analytical queries over large amounts of data. The results of analytical queries are usually calculated after an aggregation over multiple rows from one or more tables. BI applications use analytical queries to aggregate data and visualize it. It is a common architectural approach to use a data warehouse to serve data to a BI application.

Back in 2012, AWS launched **Amazon Redshift**, a cloud-native, fully managed data warehouse service. Today, Redshift is one of the most popular cloud data warehouses with thousands of organizations from different verticals using it to analyze their data. Other popular cloud data warehouses include Snowflake and Google BigQuery. Amazon Redshift integrates with most BI tools and it integrates natively with Amazon QuickSight. We will discuss this topic in more detail in *Chapter 3, Preparing Data with Amazon QuickSight*, when we look more closely into Amazon QuickSight-supported data sources.

Data lake storage and governance

A data lake is a repository of data where organizations can easily centralize all of their data and apply it in different use cases such as reporting, visualization, big data analytics, and predictive analytics. Data stored in data lakes can be structured or semi-structured. Usually, data is ingested into the data lake in its raw format, and is then transformed and stored back into the data lake for further processing and analysis. A cloud data lake typically uses a cloud object store to store data. AWS introduced **Amazon Simple Storage Service (S3)** in March 2006, offering developers a highly scalable, reliable, and low-latency data storage infrastructure at very low cost. Amazon S3 can store an unlimited amount of data, a particularly useful feature for data lakes. Organizations have one less thing to worry about because they don't need to think about scaling their storage as the amount of data stored grows.

While scaling data lake storage is something that organizations and CIOs don't need to worry about much anymore, data lake governance needs to be considered carefully. Data lakes do not enforce data schemas or data formats and, without any governance, data lakes can degrade into unusable data repositories, often referred to as **data swamps**. AWS offers a number of services for data governance.

The **AWS Glue Catalog** is part of the AWS Glue service. It is a fully managed Apache Hive metastore-compatible data catalog. Big data applications (for example, Apache Spark, Apache Hive, Presto, and so on) use the metadata in the catalog to locate and parse data. The AWS Glue Catalog is a technical metadata repository and can catalog data in Amazon S3, and a number of relational or non-relational data stores including Redshift, Aurora, and DynamoDB, among others.

AWS Lake Formation runs on top of AWS Glue and Amazon S3 and provides a governance layer and access layer for data lakes on Amazon S3. It also provides a set of reusable ETL jobs, called blueprints, that can be used to perform common ETL tasks (for example, loading data from a relational data store into an S3 data lake). Lake Formation allows users to manage access permissions, using a familiar GRANT REVOKE syntax that you might have seen in **relational database management systems (RDBMSes)**.

Amazon Macie is an AWS service for data protection. It provides an inventory of Amazon S3 buckets and it uses machine learning to identify and alert its users about sensitive data, such as **personally identifiable information (PII)**.

Finally, and perhaps most importantly, AWS **Identity and Access Management (IAM)** is a fundamental AWS service that allows users to assign permissions to principals (for example, users, groups, or roles) and explicitly allow or deny access to AWS resources including data lake locations or tables in the data catalog.

Ad hoc analytics

Ad hoc analytics refers to getting answers from the data on an as-needed basis. Contrary with what happens with scheduled reports, ad hoc querying is initiated by a user when they need to get specific answers from their data. The user typically uses SQL via a workbench type of application or other analytics frameworks (for instance, Apache Spark) using notebook environments or other BI applications. AWS has a number of analytics services that can be used for ad hoc analytics.

Amazon Redshift can be used for ad hoc analysis of data. For ad hoc querying, users will typically connect to Amazon Redshift using a query editor application with the Redshift JDBC/ODBC drivers. Notebook integrations or BI tool integrations are also possible for ad hoc analysis. AWS offers a number of managed notebook environments such as EMR notebooks and SageMaker notebooks. Amazon Redshift also allows its users to query data that is stored outside the data warehouse. Amazon Redshift Spectrum allows Redshift users to query data stored in Amazon S3, eliminating the need to load the data first before querying. Redshift's federated querying capability allows users to query live data in operational data stores such as PostgreSQL and MySQL.

For big data and data lakes, Presto is a popular choice for ad hoc analysis. Presto provides a high-performance parallel SQL query engine. **Amazon Athena** lets users run Presto queries in a scalable serverless environment. Amazon QuickSight natively supports Amazon Athena. We will talk more about this native integration in *Chapter 3, Preparing Data with Amazon QuickSight*. Amazon EMR is a fully managed Hadoop cluster, and it comes with a range of applications from the open source big data ecosystem. Presto has two community projects, PrestoSQL and PrestoDB, both of which are part of the Amazon EMR service. Other options included with EMR are Hive on EMR and Spark on EMR.

Extract, transform, load

ETL is a term used to describe a set of processes to extract, transform, and load data usually for analytical purposes. Organizations gather data from different data sources and centralize them in a central data repository. Data from different sources typically has different schemas and different conventions and standards, and therefore it can be challenging to combine them to get the required answers. For that reason, data needs to transformed so that it can work together. For example, cleaning the data, applying certain data quality thresholds, and standardizing to a specific standard (for instance, date and time formats used) are all important tasks to ensure the data is useable. A visual representation of the ETL process is shown in the following figure.

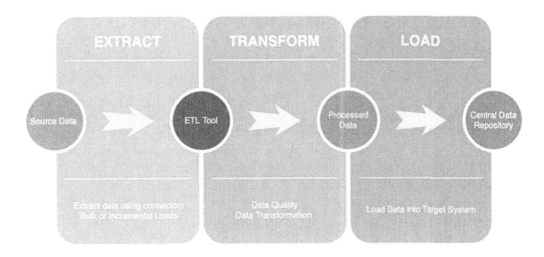

Figure 1.2 – The ETL process

AWS Glue is a fully managed ETL service offered by AWS. When it was first introduced in 2017, Glue ETL offered an Apache Spark environment optimized for ETL. Now, Glue ETL offers a wider range of options:

- **PySpark** – Apache Spark using Python
- **Spark with Scala** – Apache Spark with Scala
- **Python shell** – For smaller ETL jobs that don't need a Spark cluster
- **Glue Studio and Glue Databrew** – Visual approach to ETL without the need to write code

Amazon EMR transient clusters, with applications such as Spark or Hive, can be leveraged for ETL workloads. ETL workloads can be bulk or streaming: streaming ETL workloads usually need to be up and running constantly, or at least for as long as the source stream is on; batch ETL workloads don't need to run at all times and they can stop once the data is loaded into the target system. This type of workload fits nicely with the flexibility of the cloud. With the cloud, data architects don't need to think of Hadoop clusters as big monolithic clusters. Instead, users prefer purpose-built transient clusters, optimized and sized to handle specific workloads and data loads.

Now that we've had our overview of the AWS analytics ecosystem, let's learn about modern data architecture and how they are built.

Exploring the modern data architecture on AWS

The modern data architecture is a modern data analytics architecture: as the name suggests, it combines the **data lake** and the **data warehouse** into a seamless system. This approach extends the traditional data warehouse approach and opens up new possibilities for data analytics. For this reason, it is important to understand this architecture, which can be used as a data backend for Amazon QuickSight or other BI applications. To understand the architecture better, let's first start by understanding the differences between a data lake and data warehouse.

Data lakes versus data warehouses

Data lakes and data warehouses are designed to consume large amounts of data for analytics purposes. Data warehouses are traditional database systems, used by organizations and enterprises for years. Data lakes, on the other side, are relatively young implementations that emerged from the big data and Hadoop ecosystems. Tables stored in data warehouses need to have clearly defined schemas. The schema needs to be defined upfront, before any data is added. This approach is called **schema on write**, and it ensures that data conforms to a specific structure before being ingested into the data warehouse. However, it can be less flexible, and it may introduce complexity when dealing with evolving schemas. Evolving schemas are an increasingly common scenario because organizations need to capture more and more data points from their customer interactions to drive data-driven decisions.

On the other side, data lakes don't enforce a schema upfront. Instead, applications that have the required permissions can write data to a data lake. Structure and data formats aren't enforced by the data lake: it is a responsibility of the writing application.

Data stored in a data lake has few to no limitations regarding its format: it can be **structured**, **semi-structured**, or completely **unstructured**. For many datasets, a schema can be inferred, either because the data is semi-structured (CSV, JSON, and others), or they follow patterns that can be identified after applying regular expressions and extracting specific columns. In data lakes, the schema is inferred when the data is read by the querying application. This approach is called **schema on read**, and it gives an organization flexibility regarding the data type stored. However, it also introduces challenges with data complexity and enforcing data quality.

For that reason, it is common that data that lands into the data lake goes through a series of transformations to get to a stage where it is useable. The first stage, often referred to as the **raw** layer, is where the data first lands, and it is stored as is.

After the data has landed, the first series of transformations is applied and the data is stored at the processed layer. Since the data can be of any format, the types of possible transformations are limitless. To give just some examples, data quality functions can be applied at this stage to remove incomplete rows and standardize the data in line with a specific datetime or time zone format. Other data engineering activities can also be performed at this stage, such as converting data into different file data formats optimized for analytics, or organizing them into folders using specific information (usually temporal) that can be later used as a partition column by the querying application.

Finally, data can then be converted for specific use cases and landed into the target layer. As an example, data can be transformed in a way that is relevant for a specific machine learning algorithm to work with the data. Another use case could be BI applications, such as Amazon QuickSight, where data can be pre-joined or aggregated and therefore reduced from a large dataset into a smaller dataset that is easier to visualize. Additional data engineering can be applied at this stage to optimize for performance.

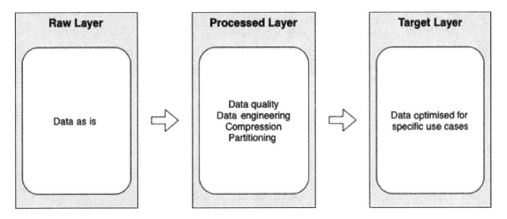

Figure 1.3 – Data lake layers

The data warehouse and data lake architectures are now being challenged by a new, hybrid type of storage: the modern data architecture.

modern data architecture on AWS

This section will look more closely at an example modern data architecture on AWS using AWS managed services. Let's start by defining the key components of the modern data architecture:

- **Amazon Redshift** is the data warehouse service.
- **Amazon S3** is the object store that can be used for cloud data lake storage.
- **AWS Glue** is the data lake catalog to store technical metadata.

> **Note**
>
> AWS Glue Catalog tables can be stored in Amazon Redshift, providing a
> unified metadata catalog across both the data warehouse and the S3 data lake.

Amazon Redshift supports functionality that allows it to interact with the data warehouse.
Let's look at those features in more detail.

Ability to query the data lake from the data warehouse

Redshift Spectrum is a feature of Redshift that allows you to perform SQL queries against
data in the S3 data lake. The queries are triggered directly from the data warehouse, and
therefore you don't need to connect to a different environment to submit your queries.
You need to define the Spectrum tables as external tables on their data warehouse. The
Redshift cluster also needs to have permission to access the data lake S3 location(s). The
Redshift cluster will need to be assigned an IAM role, which needs to have access to the
desired S3 locations.

Another key characteristic of Redshift Spectrum is that the Spectrum queries are
running in the Spectrum nodes that are outside of the Redshift cluster. This effectively
extends the Redshift cluster with additional compute capacity when data lake data needs
to be queried.

Finally, Spectrum tables and Redshift tables can be combined and joined. Without this
feature, you would have to move data and collocate it before joining it.

Ability to load data from the data lake

Redshift can efficiently load data from the S3 data lake. Specifically, Redshift's COPY
command can load data in parallel from Amazon S3. You (at a minimum) need to define
a table name, the data location (commonly S3), and the authorization to access the data in
the source location. When loading multiple files from S3, Redshift parallelizes the loading
by allocating each file to a Redshift slice (the unit of processing in Redshift).

Ability to unload data to the data lake

Redshift also comes with the ability to unload data from the data warehouse back to
the data lake. Specifically, the UNLOAD command unloads the result of the query onto
Amazon S3. You (as a minimum) need to specify the S3 location and the authorization.
There are more options, such as defining the file format (using the FORMAT AS option) or
applying partitioning (using the PARTITION BY option), and others.

In the following diagram, we see an example data pipeline that is using both a data warehouse and a data lake on AWS. Data is loaded from the operational data stores into the Amazon S3 object store in the raw layer of the data lake. Then, with a set of ETL jobs, the data reaches a stage that can be loaded into the data warehouse for BI purposes. For cost-effectiveness, you might not want to load all the data into the warehouse. Instead, you might want to leave the data in the data lake but have the ability to query the data when needed. This architecture considers the temperature of the data (how frequently the data is accessed) to determine the best storage. **Hot** data that needs to be accessed frequently is loaded into the data warehouse, while **colder** data remains in the data lake, a cheaper long-term storage option.

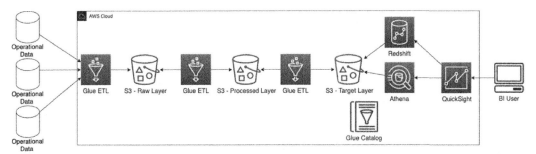

Figure 1.4 – Example data pipeline on AWS

Now that we have had an overview of the modern data architecture on AWS, let's build a basic modern data architecture on AWS.

Creating a basic modern data architecture

In this section, we will go through a hands-on example to create a basic modern data architecture. This tutorial will use the AWS CLI and the AWS console. By the end of this section, we will have spun up a working data lake and a data warehouse environment with demo data loaded.

> **Important note**
> The resources for this tutorial might introduce charges to your AWS account. Once you finish with the exercise, make sure you clean up the resources to prevent incurring further charges.

Creating the data lake storage

In this step, we will add the data lake storage. Then we will upload a demo dataset and will discover its schema automatically.

Step 1 – creating the S3 bucket

Let's begin:

1. If you haven't installed it already, follow the AWS documentation to install and configure the AWS CLI. To complete this tutorial, you will need to use a role that has access to the S3, Glue, Redshift, and IAM services: `https://docs.aws.amazon.com/cli/latest/userguide/cli-chap-configure.html`.

2. First, let's create the S3 bucket as the data lake storage. Your S3 bucket needs to have a globally unique name. For that reason, we should introduce some randomness to it. Let's pick a random set of 10 characters and numbers. For this tutorial, you should choose your own random set of characters for this string; for example, `SF482XHS7M`.

   We will use the random string in the data lake name, to ensure it is globally unique.

   Let's use `my-data-lake-<random string>` as the bucket name.

3. To create a bucket, we can type the following command into the CLI. Replace the following random string with your random string:

   ```
   % aws s3api create-bucket --bucket data-lake-xxxxxxxxx
   --region us-east-1
   ```

   And the response should look like this:

   ```
   {
        "Location": "/data-lake-xxxxxxxxx"
   }
   ```

Step 2 – adding data into the data lake

Now let's add some data. For this exercise, we will use a subset of the New York City **Taxi and Limousine Commission** (**TLC**) Trip Record Data:

1. Let's first have a look at the dataset:

   ```
   % aws s3 ls 's3://nyc-tlc/trip data/' --no-sign-request
   ```

   This command will return all the files in the open S3 location:

   ```
   2016-08-11 15:32:21     85733063 fhv_tripdata_2015-01.csv
   2016-08-11 15:33:04     97863482 fhv_tripdata_2015-02.csv
   2016-08-11 15:33:40    102220197 fhv_tripdata_2015-03.csv
   ...
   2021-02-26 16:54:00    138989555 yellow_tripdata_2020-11.
   csv
   ```

```
2021-02-26 16:54:00  134481400 yellow_tripdata_2020-12.
csv
```

We don't need to download all of them. For this tutorial, we will copy only the files for 2020.

2. We can use the S3 CLI `exclude` and `include` parameters to apply a pattern to match the desired filenames. The command to copy is as follows:

```
% aws s3 cp "s3://nyc-tlc/trip data/" s3://data-lake-
xxxxxxxxxx/yellowtrips/ --recursive --exclude "*"
--include "yellow_tripdata_2020*"
```

3. Once completed, we can then verify that the files exist in our environment with the `aws s3 ls` command, which lists the files under a specific S3 location:

```
% aws s3 ls s3://data-lake-xxxxxxxxxx/yellowtrips/
2021-03-27 16:53:41  593610736 yellow_tripdata_2020-01.
csv
2021-03-27 16:53:41  584190585 yellow_tripdata_2020-02.
csv
2021-03-27 16:53:42  278288608 yellow_tripdata_2020-03.
csv
2021-03-27 16:53:41   21662261 yellow_tripdata_2020-04.
csv
2021-03-27 16:53:43   31641590 yellow_tripdata_2020-05.
csv
2021-03-27 16:53:42   50277193 yellow_tripdata_2020-06.
csv
2021-03-27 16:53:44   73326707 yellow_tripdata_2020-07.
csv
2021-03-27 16:53:46   92411545 yellow_tripdata_2020-08.
csv
2021-03-27 16:53:50  123394595 yellow_tripdata_2020-09.
csv
2021-03-27 16:53:54  154917592 yellow_tripdata_2020-10.
csv
2021-03-27 16:53:57  138989555 yellow_tripdata_2020-11.
csv
2021-03-27 16:53:58  134481400 yellow_tripdata_2020-12.
csv
```

> **Note**
> You can use data in a shared data lake as part of your data lake without the need to actually copy it across to your data lake.

Step 3 – identifying the schema

The next step is to identify the schema of the dataset. For this purpose, we will use the AWS Glue crawlers. AWS Glue crawlers crawl through the data to detect the schema. If a schema can be determined (remember there is no guarantee that the data has a specific schema) then Glue crawlers will populate the Glue Catalog with the schemas identified after crawling the data. Glue tables always belong to a Glue database. A database in Glue is just a logical repository of tables in the Glue Catalog:

1. Let's start by creating a database using the `create-database` command:

    ```
    % aws glue create-database --database-input
    "{\"Name\":\"my-data-lake-db\"}" --region us-east-1
    ```

2. We can verify the successful database creation using the `get-databases` command:

    ```
    % aws glue get-databases --region us-east-1
    {
        "DatabaseList": [
            {
                "Name": "default",
                "CreateTime": 1553517157.0
            },

            {
                "Name": "my-data-lake-db",
                "CreateTime": 1616865129.0
            }
        ]
    }
    ```

3. Before we create the Glue Crawler, we need to create an IAM role that will be assigned to the Crawler and allow it to access the data in the data lake. The crawler doesn't need to write to the data lake location, therefore only the read access permission is needed. To give the required permissions to a role, we need to attach policies that define the permissions. Let's define a policy document that allows read access to our data lake:

```
{
    "Version": "2012-10-17",
    "Statement": [
        {
            "Effect": "Allow",
            "Action": [
                "s3:GetObject",
                "s3:ListBucket"
            ],
            "Resource": [
                "arn:aws:s3:::data-lake-xxxxxxxxxx",
                "arn:aws:s3:::data-lake-xxxxxxxxxx/*"
            ]
        }
    ]
}
```

The preceding policy document allows the policy holder to use the S3 `ListBucket` and the `GetObject` API. The crawler will use `ListBucket` to list the objects in our data lake bucket and `getObject` to read objects as it crawls data. This policy restricts access to the data lake bucket only.

4. Now, let's create a file and copy the policy text. Replace the random string in the data lake name with the random string in your environment. I used `vim`, but you can use any text editor:

```
% vim policy
```

5. Then, let's create the IAM policy using the `create-policy` CLI command:

```
% aws iam create-policy --policy-name DataLakeReadAccess
--policy-document file://policy
```

The preceding command created the policy and we should get a confirmation JSON object back. Note the **policy ARN**, as we will use it in a later step.

6. Next, let's create the IAM role that the Glue crawler will assume. First, let's define the role policy document:

```
{
            "Version": "2012-10-17",
            "Statement": [
                {
                        "Action": "sts:AssumeRole",
                        "Effect": "Allow",
                        "Principal": {
                                "Service": "glue.amazonaws.com"
                        }
                }
            ]
}
```

7. Then create a file called `role-policy` and copy in the preceding JSON document:

```
% vim role-policy
```

This role policy document allows the Glue service to assume the role we will create.

8. To create the role, we will use the `iam create-role` CLI command:

```
% aws iam create-role --role-name GlueCrawlerRole
--assume-role-policy-document file://role-policy
```

We should get a confirmation JSON message after running the command.

9. Capture the role ARN, as it will be used later when defining the crawler.

10. Then, let's attach the required policies to this role. For this role, we want to allocate two policies: the `AWSGlueServiceRole` policy (this is managed by AWS) and the `DataLakeReadAccess` policy we created earlier. To attach policies to the IAM role we will use the `iam attach-role-policy` command. Let's start with the `AWSGlueServiceRole` policy:

```
% aws iam attach-role-policy --role-name GlueCrawlerRole
--policy-arn arn:aws:iam::aws:policy/service-role/
AWSGlueServiceRole
```

11. Then we will attach the `DataLakeReadAccess` policy. We will need the policy ARN that we captured earlier. The policy ARN should look like the following line:

```
arn:aws:iam::<accountid>:policy/DataLakeReadAccess
```

And the command should look like the following:

```
% aws iam attach-role-policy --role-name GlueCrawlerRole
--policy-arn arn:aws:iam::<ACCOUNT-ID>:policy/
DataLakeReadAccess
```

12. Now, let's create the AWS Glue crawler. For this purpose, we will use the `glue create-crawler` CLI command. Make sure you replace the role ARN and the data lake location with the values for your environment:

```
% aws glue create-crawler --name qs-book-crawler
--role arn:aws:iam::xxxxxxxxxxxx:role/GlueCrawlerRole
--database-name my-data-lake-db --targets
"{\"S3Targets\":[{\"Path\":\"s3://data-lake-xxxxxxxxxx/
yellowtrips\"}]}" --region us-east-1
```

13. Then, just start the crawler using the `glue start-crawler` command:

```
% aws glue start-crawler --name qs-book-crawler --region
us-east-1
```

After 1-2 minutes, the Glue crawler should populate the database.

14. We can confirm this by calling the `glue get-tables cli` command:

```
% aws glue get-tables --database-name my-data-lake-db
```

15. You can view the Catalog from the AWS Console. Log in to the AWS Console and navigate to AWS Glue.

16. Then on the left-hand side menu, under **Data Catalog**, choose **Databases** and then find `my-data-lake-db`. Then click on **View tables** under `my-data-lake-db`. It should look like the following screenshot:

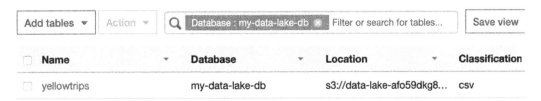

Name	Database	Location	Classification
yellowtrips	my-data-lake-db	s3://data-lake-afo59dkg8...	csv

Figure 1.5 – Glue console

> **Tip**
>
> You can click the checkbox to select the table and then, under **Action**, you can choose **Preview Data**. This will open the Amazon Athena console and run an Athena query that returns 10 values from the table.

Step 4 – creating the data warehouse

Let's create our data warehouse next.

To create the data warehouse, we will use the `redshift create-cluster` CLI command, or you can use the AWS Console:

```
%aws redshift create-cluster --node-type dc2.large --number-of-
nodes 2 --master-username admin --master-user-password R3dsh1ft
--cluster-identifier mycluster --region us-east-1
```

This command should give a response with the cluster metadata. After a few minutes, our cluster will be up and running.

> **Note**
>
> This command will create a Redshift cluster with a public IP address. This is something that should be avoided in real-world scenarios. The instructions provided are oversimplified for the purposes of this tutorial as this book is not focused on Amazon Redshift.

Step 5 – loading the data into the data warehouse

First, let's create an IAM role that we will assign to the Redshift cluster. We will use this role when using the Redshift Spectrum feature to query data in S3. We want the cluster to be able to write and read to our S3 location. We also want the cluster to be able to have read access to the Glue Catalog:

1. Similarly to what we did earlier, we will create the following role policy document to allow the role to be assumed by the Redshift service:

```
{
        "Version": "2012-10-17",
        "Statement": [
            {
                "Action": "sts:AssumeRole",
```

```
            "Effect": "Allow",
            "Principal": {
                "Service": "redshift.amazonaws.
com"
            }
        }
    ]
}
```

2. Then copy this JSON object into a policy document:

```
% vim role-policy-redshift
```

3. Now, let's create the role using the `iam create-role` command:

```
% aws iam create-role --role-name RedshiftSpectrumRole
--assume-role-policy-document file://role-policy-redshift
```

Note the role ARN, as we will use it later to attach it to the cluster.

4. Next, we need to give the desired permissions by attaching the correct policies. This time, for simplicity, we will just attach two AWS managed policies. These policies are overly permissive, and normally we would attach policies with narrower permissions, as we did for the Glue crawlers in *Step 3*. Let's attach `AWSFullS3Access` and `AWSFullGlueAccess`:

```
% aws iam attach-role-policy --role-
name RedshiftSpectrumRole --policy-arn
arn:aws:iam::aws:policy/AmazonS3FullAccess
% aws iam attach-role-policy --role-
name RedshiftSpectrumRole --policy-arn
arn:aws:iam::aws:policy/AWSGlueConsoleFullAccess
```

5. Next, we will attach this role to our cluster using the `redshift modify-cluster-iam-roles` CLI command. Note that you need to update the role ARN with the value from your environment:

```
% aws redshift modify-cluster-iam-roles
--cluster-identifier mycluster --add-iam-roles
arn:aws:iam::<ACCOUNT-ID>:role/RedshiftSpectrumRole
--region us-east-1
```

6. The cluster change will take a few minutes to be applied. After the change is applied, the cluster will be ready to fetch data from the S3 data lake. To connect to the cluster, we will use the built-in **query editor** found in the AWS Management Console. To find the editor, navigate to the Redshift console, and see the left-hand side menu. The editor will need to establish a connection. Make sure you select the cluster we created earlier, and type dev as the database name and admin as the username.

> **Note**
>
> We didn't set a database name earlier. Redshift uses dev as the default value.

7. In the editor page, we will need to create a table to store the data. Let's name the table yellowtrips_3mo, as we will only store 3 months' worth of data:

```
create table yellowtrips_3mo
(vendorid varchar(10),
tpep_pickup_datetime datetime,
tpep_dropoff_datetime datetime,
passenger_count int,
trip_distance float,
ratecodeid varchar(10),
store_and_fwd_flag char(1),
pulocationid varchar(10),
dolocationid varchar(10),
payment_type varchar(10),
fare_amount float,
extra float,
mta_tax float,
tip_amount float,
tolls_amount float,
improvement_surcharge float,
total_amount float,
congestion_surcharge float);
```

8. Then, let's copy 3 months' worth of data into the data warehouse. Let's use the COPY command, as follows:

```
copy yellowtrips_3mo from
's3://data-lake-afo59dkg84/yellowtrips/yellow_
tripdata_2020-10.csv'
iam_role 'arn:aws:iam::xxxxxxxxxxxx:role/
RedshiftSpectrumRole' FORMAT AS CSV dateformat 'auto'
ignoreheader 1;
copy yellowtrips_3mo from
's3://data-lake-afo59dkg84/yellowtrips/yellow_
tripdata_2020-11.csv'
iam_role 'arn:aws:iam::xxxxxxxxxxxx:role/
RedshiftSpectrumRole' FORMAT AS CSV dateformat 'auto'
ignoreheader 1;
copy yellowtrips_3mo from
's3://data-lake-afo59dkg84/yellowtrips/yellow_
tripdata_2020-12.csv'
iam_role 'arn:aws:iam::xxxxxxxxxxxx:role/
RedshiftSpectrumRole' FORMAT AS CSV dateformat 'auto'
ignoreheader 1;
```

9. At this stage, we have a data lake with 12 months' worth of data and a data warehouse that contains only the most recent data (3 months). One of the characteristics of the modern data architecture is that it allows its users to query the data lake from the data warehouse. Feel free to query the data and start getting an understanding of the dataset. Let's create the external schema so that we can enable the Spectrum feature. Use the following command in your Redshift editor. Replace the role ARN with the values from your environment:

```
create external schema spectrum_schema from data catalog
database 'my-data-lake-db'
iam_role 'arn:aws:iam::xxxxxxxxxxxx:role/
RedshiftSpectrumRole'
create external database if not exists;
```

10. Let's just compare the size of the two tables using a simple count(*) query:

```
select count(*) from public.yellowtrips_3mo;
select count(*) from spectrum_schema.yellowtrips;
```

The first query will run against the recent data in the data warehouse. The second will run against the first query using the Spectrum nodes using the data in the data lake. As expected, the number of records in the data lake should be much higher than the number of records in the data warehouse. Specifically, the query result was 24,648,499 for the year 2020 and 4,652,013 records for the last 3 months of 2020.

> **Note**
>
> The Spectrum queries use the Spectrum nodes and are charged separately from the Redshift cluster. Every query incurs an added cost based on the data it needs to scan. Refer to the AWS pricing for details.

Feel free to experiment with the data and trigger a few queries to understand the dataset. When you finish with the Redshift cluster, you can **pause** the cluster so that you stop the on-demand billing. Once the cluster is paused you will only pay for the cluster storage.

Summary

Congratulations, you have reached the end of the first chapter! By now, you should have a good understanding of the AWS analytics ecosystem and its data lake and data warehousing options. In this chapter, we discussed in detail the key differences between data warehouses and data lakes. We also discussed the modern data architecture on AWS, and we looked at its main components in more detail. Finally, during the step-by-step section in this chapter, you had a chance to create a data lake and a data warehouse from scratch, and you loaded an open dataset for further analysis later on. We also defined Spectrum tables and queried the data lake directly for the data warehouse.

In the next chapter, we will discuss the basic concepts of Amazon QuickSight, understand its main benefits, and learn how to set up a QuickSight account.

Questions

1. What is the difference between data lakes and data warehouses?
2. What is schema on read and what is schema on write?
3. How can we identify the schema of new data in a data lake on AWS?
4. Which AWS storage service is ideal for a data lake on AWS?
5. What data is better served from the data lake in the modern data architecture?
6. How do Redshift Spectrum tables differ from Redshift tables?

Further reading

- *Big Data and Analytics Options on AWS* – 2018 – AWS whitepaper: `https://d0.awsstatic.com/whitepapers/Big_Data_Analytics_Options_on_AWS.pdf`

- *Cloud Native Data Virtualization on AWS* – 2020 – AWS whitepaper: `https://d1.awsstatic.com/whitepapers/cloud-native-data-virtualization-on-aws.pdf?did=wp_card&trk=wp_card`

2

Introduction to Amazon QuickSight

In this chapter, we will introduce **Amazon QuickSight** and we will define its main components. We will discuss fundamental architectural topics such as networking and storage, and look closely at the different editions of Amazon QuickSight and understand the different options available during account creation. Finally, we will walk through a step-by-step guide to set up a QuickSight account, and configure the QuickSight permissions to access data in a data lake.

To summarize, in this chapter, we will cover the following:

- Introducing Amazon QuickSight
- Introducing QuickSight editions and user authorization options
- Setting up Amazon QuickSight

Technical requirements

The only thing you will need for this chapter is an AWS account.

Introducing Amazon QuickSight

Amazon QuickSight is a **business intelligence (BI)** cloud-native service. BI developers use QuickSight to develop data visualizations and dashboards and report the state of the business. Being cloud-native **BI** software, QuickSight can scale to thousands of users without the need to provision additional compute capacity. In fact, the concept of compute capacity doesn't exist in QuickSight: AWS is responsible for scaling QuickSight up or down when demand grows or shrinks, while BI developers focus on developing data visualizations.

Next, we will define the following core concepts of QuickSight:

- Datasets
- Analysis
- Visuals and insights
- Dashboards

Datasets

QuickSight datasets are the data imported into QuickSight for visualization; a dataset can be built from one or more data sources. Amazon QuickSight supports a number of data sources. Datasets can either be cached in QuickSight (SPICE, which we will cover later in this chapter) or query the data source directly. We will discuss data sources and data preparation in more detail in *Chapter 3, Preparing Data with Amazon QuickSight*.

> **Note**
>
> Datasets and data sources are different concepts in QuickSight. A dataset can consist of one or more data sources. Typically, a degree of data preparation is applied to a data source before it becomes a dataset.

Analysis

An analysis in QuickSight refers to the editing part of the application, typically used by a BI developer to build their visualizations. We will see how to create an analysis in *Chapter 4, Developing Visuals and Dashboards*.

> **Note**
> A QuickSight analysis can be developed against one or more datasets.

Visuals and insights

A QuickSight analysis consists of onscreen components/widgets that contain data visualizations. A BI developer can add two different types of these components:

- Visuals
- Insights

Visuals are graphical representations of a dataset commonly using plot types and charts. Other visual types include tables (simple or pivot), geospatial visualizations such as maps, and others. We will cover the various visual types in detail in *Chapter 4, Developing Visuals and Dashboards*.

> Tip
> QuickSight has a special visual type called **AutoGraph**. It appears with the ⚡ symbol. When selected, QuickSight automatically identifies and applies the most appropriate visual type for the data types and fields selected.

Insights are special components that use common analytical or ML functions to provide insights into data. The result of an insight appears in natural language. Amazon QuickSight provides both pre-built insights and customizable insights. We will talk more about QuickSight insights in *Chapter 6, Working with ML Capabilities and Insights*.

Dashboards

Once an analysis is developed and ready to be published, a BI developer can export it into a QuickSight dashboard. A dashboard is a read-only version of an analysis. A dashboard is typically accessed by business users and shared by BI developers for reporting reasons. A BI developer can also add custom controls and add interactivity to their dashboards. We will cover QuickSight dashboards in detail in *Chapter 4, Developing Visuals and Dashboards*.

Next, we will define the different user roles found in Amazon QuickSight.

Introducing Amazon QuickSight user types

QuickSight supports three different user types:

- Admin
- Author
- Reader

Admin

The QuickSight **admin** role can perform both administrative tasks and BI development tasks. A QuickSight account can have one or more users with the admin role assigned. The admin user role can do the following:

- Manage users
- Manage QuickSight settings and subscriptions
- Manage connections and storage
- Whitelist domains for dashboard embedding
- Configure **single sign-on** (SSO)

> **Note**
>
> Admins are *not* superusers in Amazon QuickSight and they don't gain automatic access to analyses or dashboards created by other users.

Author

In QuickSight, **author** is the role needed for BI developers to build datasets and analyses. The author role can do the following:

- Create datasets
- Create and develop analyses
- Share analyses
- Publish dashboards to users

Reader

In QuickSight, **reader** is the role for business users to consume dashboards. The reader role can do the following:

- Log in to the QuickSight mobile or web app
- Receive email alerts
- Access and view dashboards
- Use a dashboard's predefined onscreen controls

The following table summarizes the differences between the three different user roles.

	READER	AUTHOR	ADMIN
ACCESS QUICKSIGHT	√	√	√
RECEIVE ALERTS	√	√	√
USE DASHBOARDS	√	√	√
CREATE DATASETS		√	√
CREATE ANALYSIS		√	√
SHARE ANALYSIS		√	√
MANAGE USERS			√
MANAGE QUICKSIGHT			√
MANAGE STORAGE			√

Figure 2.1 – QuickSight user role permissions

Putting it all together

In the following diagram, we see the end-to-end BI process with Amazon QuickSight. We start from the data sources on the left. Data sources can be relational databases, data warehouses, APIs from SaaS vendors, or data from a data lake and files. From these data sources, an author (BI developer) can configure datasets, which can then be used for creating QuickSight analyses. When an analysis is ready, the BI developer can share it as a dashboard with other business users. The business users can then access the dashboard via their web browsers or their mobile phones, and drive business decisions using data.

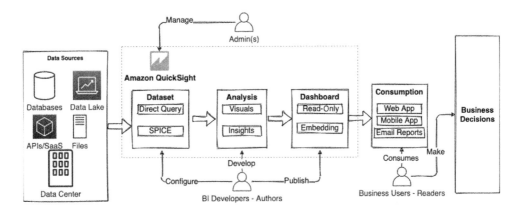

Figure 2.2 – QuickSight end-to-end process

Now that we have introduced the main components of QuickSight, we will look more closely into its architectural concepts, such as networking and storage.

Introducing QuickSight architecture

QuickSight is a fully managed service that runs exclusively on the AWS cloud. QuickSight visualizations can be consumed either via QuickSight for the web, the QuickSight mobile app, or can be embedded into a custom application. Embedded analytics will be covered in more detail in *Chapter 7, Understanding Embedded Analytics*. QuickSight is centrally hosted, which means that AWS is responsible for scaling and managing the underlying infrastructure, allowing users to focus on developing BI applications. QuickSight is licensed on a subscription basis according to the number of users or sessions.

In this section, we will cover a few fundamental topics of the QuickSight architecture. These will cover the basic networking concepts and storage.

Introducing QuickSight networking concepts

In this section, we will cover fundamental networking topics that will help us understand how to architect with QuickSight. Networking is an important concept when you configure your data sources because QuickSight will need to establish a working connection to either query the data source or load data from the source into the QuickSight service.

AWS **Virtual Private Cloud** (**VPC**) is a logically isolated virtual network on the AWS cloud. Organizations that need to achieve workload isolation use AWS VPC to create a virtual network to host their workloads. Analytical databases, such as data warehouses, are commonly hosted on a VPC configured to block inbound internet connectivity. BI applications that need to connect to those data sources will need to have a network route to them. In Amazon QuickSight, admins can configure VPC connectivity. Once configured, Amazon QuickSight will automatically set up a QuickSight elastic network interface inside your VPC. An **elastic network interfacenterface** (**ENI**) is the equivalent of a virtual network card.

Only data sources that have been configured to use the VPC connection will use the interface. Using this connection, you can access a data source with a private IP address, without internet access. The following diagram shows the network configuration when connecting QuickSight to a VPC data store.

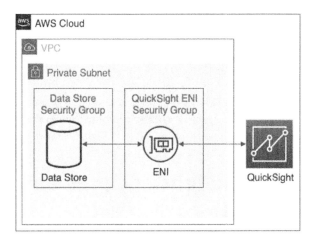

Figure 2.3 – VPC connectivity with Amazon QuickSight

Now that we have discussed the networking fundamentals, we will talk about SPICE, the QuickSight managed storage technology.

Introducing SPICE

Super-fast Parellel In-memory Calculation Engine (**SPICE**) is an important concept in Amazon QuickSight that can speed up QuickSight performance while reducing costs. You can import data into SPICE and use it as a caching layer between your data source and QuickSight. BI applications make it possible to trigger many queries at one time, some of which can be expensive. Typically, analytical queries scan and aggregate a large number of rows, and this can be computationally intensive. However, when datasets are imported into SPICE, you avoid direct queries against the data source. Instead, data is served by SPICE, which is optimized to run analytical queries. Data imported into SPICE can be reused by multiple dashboards and users, eliminating the need to scale the underlying database or the data warehouse. If the data source is a pay-per-query type, such as Amazon Athena, then SPICE will introduce direct cost benefits, as it will reduce the number of queries needed to run the BI application. The data sources will only need to serve data imports into SPICE, and not the analytical queries to populate the visuals.

Capacity planning for SPICE storage is the responsibility of the QuickSight admin. Each AWS Region has a separate SPICE capacity. AWS provides a formula to calculate the size of SPICE capacity for a data source. The overall capacity is determined by the following:

- The number of rows
- The number of columns
- The type of columns

For each numeric or date column, QuickSight needs 8 bytes of SPICE storage. For text columns, SPICE needs 8 bytes plus the number of UTF-8 encoded characters in the text. Once you estimate how much data will be needed for one row, you can then multiply that by the total number of rows to find the total SPICE capacity required for a data source.

Now that we have looked at the fundamental networking and storage concepts of Amazon QuickSight, we will look into the different QuickSight editions and account creation options, which will be useful when setting up a QuickSight account later on.

Introducing QuickSight editions and user authorization options

In this section, we will discuss the QuickSight editions and authorization options. These are choices we will need to make first when creating a QuickSight account.

QuickSight editions

Amazon QuickSight is offered in two editions:

- **Standard edition**: The QuickSight Standard version contains the basic QuickSight functionality. The concepts of an author and a reader user role don't apply in the Standard edition. For every registered user, bundled SPICE capacity is included, and additional SPICE capacity can be purchased.

- **Enterprise edition**: The Enterprise edition offers the full functionality of Amazon QuickSight. The concept of a reader user is only applicable in the Enterprise edition of QuickSight. Every author user is bundled with SPICE storage. For reader users, Amazon QuickSight has pay-per-session pricing capped to a maximum price point per month. ML Insights, forecasting, and embedded dashboards are only available in the Enterprise edition of QuickSight.

> **Note**
>
> There are certain features, including forecasting, ML Insights, and dashboard embedding and AD integration, that aren't supported in the Standard edition and are only available with the Enterprise edition.

Choosing between editions

For some users, the Standard version might suffice to try the basic functions of Amazon QuickSight and get familiar with the user interface and the look and feel. However, the Standard edition does not offer the full functionality of QuickSight. Given that a subscription to the Enterprise version can be stopped at any time, without any commitment, the Enterprise edition might be the best starting point for the majority of use cases. For this book, we will choose the QuickSight Enterprise edition, as we will be using features only found in the Enterprise edition.

Now that we have seen the different options for QuickSight editions, we will discuss the different options for user authorization.

User authorization with QuickSight

In this section, we will look more closely into user authorization options for Amazon QuickSight. This concept is more relevant to AWS administrators, who are responsible for setting up the QuickSight subscription. During QuickSight setup, the administrator will need to select the method to authenticate QuickSight users.

First, let's examine the required permissions needed to set up an Amazon QuickSight account. The AWS principal who sets up a QuickSight account will need to have permissions to call the QuickSight API. An AWS administrator (assuming that they have the `AdministratorAccess` managed policy) can set up a QuickSight subscription as they inherit full access to the QuickSight API. However, if another user needs to set up a QuickSight subscription, then they will need to be explicitly allowed to call the required QuickSight API actions. For example, the `QuickSight:Subscribe` action is needed to subscribe to QuickSight and `QuickSight:CreateAdmin` to create a QuickSight administrator. The full list of API actions that are allowed will depend on the actions a user needs to be allowed. If you don't explicitly allow an API action for a user, then **deny** is the AWS IAM default behavior.

When you set up Amazon QuickSight Enterprise edition, you will need to specify how your users will connect to the service. QuickSight offers the following two options:

- **Use Role Based Federation (SSO)**
- **Use Active Directory**

Once configured, you can invite your users, either via email or via their federated logins, or via Active Directory if you have an Active Directory QuickSight account. When inviting users, you can choose to use AWS IAM user authentication credentials, or create brand-new credentials for QuickSight.

Now that we have looked at the basic concepts of Amazon QuickSight and understood its account creation options, let's set up an Amazon QuickSight account.

Setting up Amazon QuickSight

In this part of the book, we will create an Amazon QuickSight account. By the end of this section, you will have set up the following:

- A QuickSight Enterprise account
- An author user
- A reader user

This part of the book will be completed using the QuickSight user interface and the AWS Management Console:

1. To access QuickSight, first log in to the **AWS Management Console**. You will need to use a principal with elevated access. Since this is a non-production account, you can use an IAM user with the AdministratorAccess policy attached.

2. Then, find and select **Amazon QuickSight**, located under the **Analytics** category. If this is a brand-new account that doesn't have Amazon QuickSight set up, we will get a prompt to sign up for the service. Select **Sign up for QuickSight**.

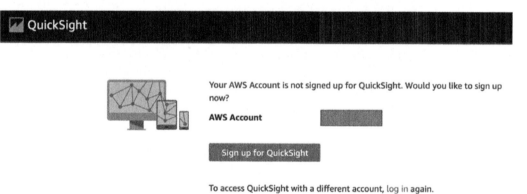

Figure 2.4 – Sign up for QuickSight

3. Then, we will see the main options for account creation. First, we will need to choose between the Standard or the Enterprise version of QuickSight. For this book, we will choose the Enterprise version. Once selected, we will need to enter the main settings to create the account.

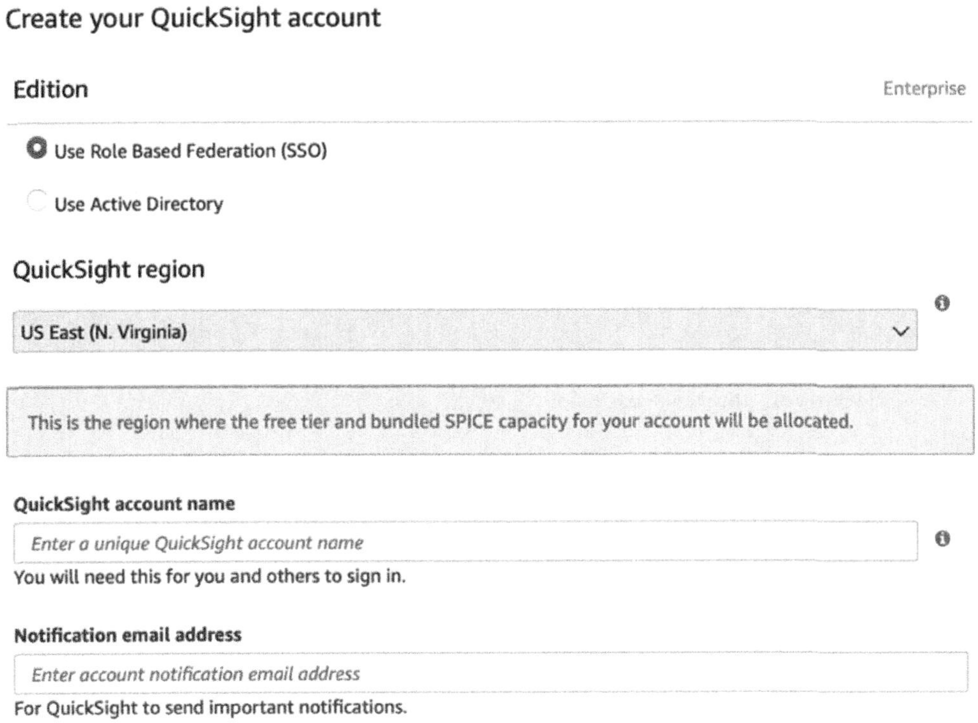

Create your QuickSight account

Edition

Enterprise

- ○ Use Role Based Federation (SSO)
- ○ Use Active Directory

QuickSight region

US East (N. Virginia)   ⌄

This is the region where the free tier and bundled SPICE capacity for your account will be allocated.

QuickSight account name

Enter a unique QuickSight account name

You will need this for you and others to sign in.

Notification email address

Enter account notification email address

For QuickSight to send important notifications.

Figure 2.5 – Account creation options

4. We will choose **Use Role Based Federation (SSO)** (instead of **Use Active Directory**).

5. Then, we will select our home region for this QuickSight account. You can go ahead with the default **US East (N. Virginia)** or pick a different region if your data sources are located in another region.

> **Note**
>
> It is preferable for QuickSight and the data sources to be in the same AWS Region. Apart from networking costs and latency reasons, QuickSight has the **autodiscovery** feature, which allows QuickSight to discover data sources within the same AWS Region, saving you time and effort when configuring data sources.

6. Then, type the QuickSight account name and an email address to receive important notifications about this QuickSight account.

> **Note**
>
> The account name needs to be globally **unique**. The account name will be used by your users to log in to Amazon QuickSight.

Then, scroll down to get to the remaining options.

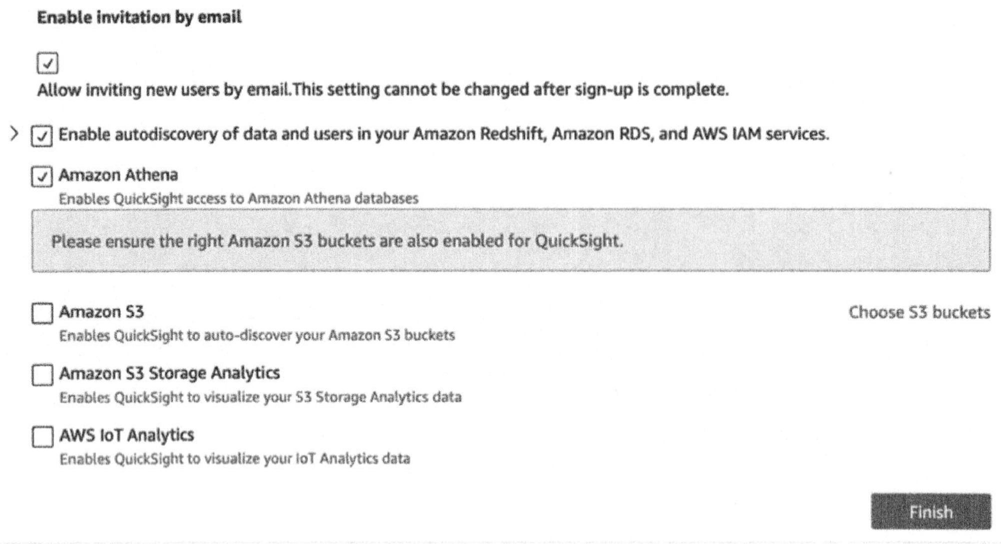

Enable invitation by email

☑
Allow inviting new users by email. This setting cannot be changed after sign-up is complete.

> ☑ Enable autodiscovery of data and users in your Amazon Redshift, Amazon RDS, and AWS IAM services.

☑ **Amazon Athena**
   Enables QuickSight access to Amazon Athena databases

   Please ensure the right Amazon S3 buckets are also enabled for QuickSight.

☐ **Amazon S3**   Choose S3 buckets
   Enables QuickSight to auto-discover your Amazon S3 buckets

☐ **Amazon S3 Storage Analytics**
   Enables QuickSight to visualize your S3 Storage Analytics data

☐ **AWS IoT Analytics**
   Enables QuickSight to visualize your IoT Analytics data

                                                                                        [Finish]

Figure 2.6 – Remaining options during account sign-up

7. Leave everything as is, and check to enable Amazon S3 access. This will allow the QuickSight service to access a specific S3 bucket in your account.

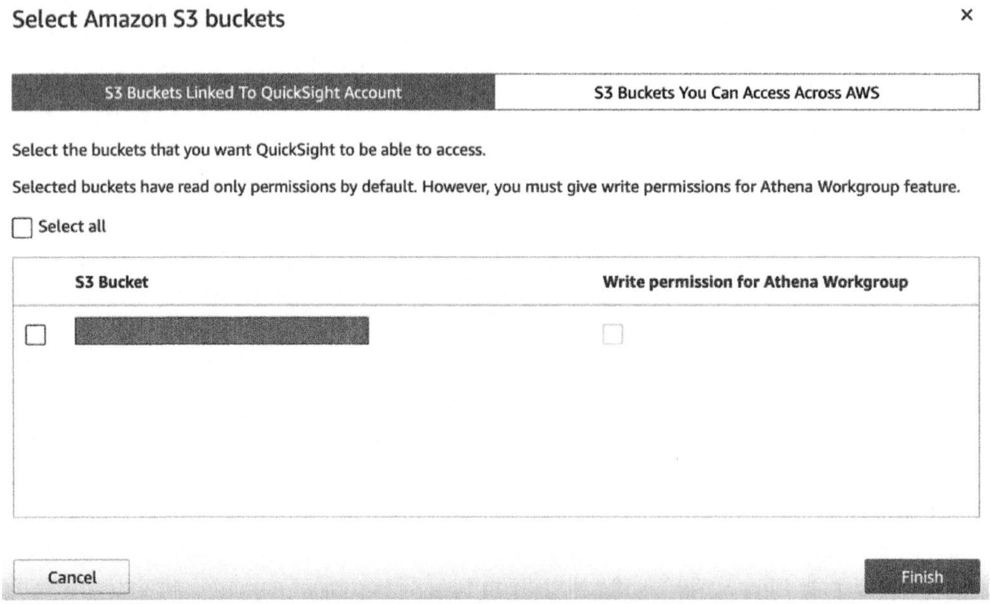

Select Amazon S3 buckets   ✕

| S3 Buckets Linked To QuickSight Account | S3 Buckets You Can Access Across AWS |

Select the buckets that you want QuickSight to be able to access.

Selected buckets have read only permissions by default. However, you must give write permissions for Athena Workgroup feature.

☐ Select all

S3 Bucket	Write permission for Athena Workgroup
☐ ▓▓▓▓▓▓▓▓▓▓▓▓▓▓▓	☐

[Cancel]   [Finish]

Figure 2.7 – Enable access to S3 buckets

8. At this stage, the screen should look like the preceding figure. You should be able to view the S3 bucket you created earlier, in *Chapter 1*, *Introducing the AWS Analytics Ecosystem*. Check **S3 Bucket** and click **Finish**. This step will automatically configure the permissions that will allow QuickSight to access your S3 bucket. Click **Finish** again to create the account.

    Congratulations! Your QuickSight account is being created and you can navigate to the home page of your account.

    Now, let's configure the first two users. One user will be allocated the author role and the other the reader role. These users will be used later in the book.

9. To invite new users, you need to navigate to the QuickSight settings. Click on your username in the top-right corner of your screen, then select **Manage QuickSight**.

> **Note**
>
> Depending on the configurations you need to perform, you might need to select a specific region before you navigate to QuickSight Management. Some configurations are only available in the **us-east-1** region and others only in your QuickSight home region.

10. After you select **Manage QuickSight**, select the **User Management** option to invite users. Click the **Invite Users** button.

11. Then we will add your two QuickSight users. Type the username you want as the first user and select **READER** or **AUTHOR** from the drop-down menu depending on the user you configure. You will also need to enter an email address for each user. This will be used to send the user invitation email. The following screenshot shows what the user invitation page looks like after configuring the two users.

Figure 2.8 – User invitation form

12. Once you fill in the user invitation form, click **Invite**. Your users will receive an invitation at the invitation email address where they can verify their email address and set up a new password to access QuickSight.

> **Note**
>
> You can also use IAM user credentials. You can select this option at the user invitation stage using the IAM user checkbox.

After your users respond to the invitation, they will be able to log in to Amazon QuickSight. You now have an Amazon QuickSight account, with an author and a reader user. You also have an admin user who was used to sign up for the QuickSight account.

Summary

Congratulations on completing this chapter! In this chapter, we introduced Amazon QuickSight and we defined its main concepts and its terminology. We explored the differences between the different QuickSight editions and we looked closely at the options during account creation. We also looked at networking and storage concepts and we discussed the different user roles: admin, author, and reader. In the last part of this chapter, you had a step-by-step guide on how to create a QuickSight account and how to invite your first users. We addressed some of the key topics that are essential to understand when working with QuickSight. We will be using this knowledge throughout this book.

In the next chapter, we will use our QuickSight account and its author user to configure data sources and datasets.

Questions

1. What are the different editions of Amazon QuickSight?
2. What is the difference between an analysis and a dashboard in QuickSight?
3. What is SPICE?
4. How can we calculate how much SPICE storage is needed?
5. How can the QuickSight admin invite users to a QuickSight account?

Further reading

- *QuickSight User Guide* – AWS: https://docs.aws.amazon.com/QuickSight/latest/user/amazon-QuickSight-user.pdf

3
Preparing Data with Amazon QuickSight

In this chapter, we will focus on QuickSight data source and dataset configurations. We will provide a step-by-step guide to set up a dataset using the data we configured in *Chapter 1, Introducing the AWS Analytics Ecosystem*. Then we will focus on using the data editor in QuickSight to edit datasets. Next, we will explore advanced dataset operations, such as the use of calculated fields and join operations. Finally, we will understand how to set up security controls.

In summary, we will learn how to do the following in this chapter:

- Adding QuickSight data sources
- Editing QuickSight datasets
- Working with advanced operations
- Configuring security controls

Technical requirements

For this chapter, you will need the following:

- An AWS account.

- A QuickSight account with the Author user configured.

- For certain sections of this chapter, we will use the architecture created in *Chapter 1, Introduction to the AWS Analytics Ecosystem*.

Adding QuickSight data sources

In this section, we will learn how to add and configure data sources with Amazon QuickSight. QuickSight supports a number of data sources. We will begin by listing the supported data sources.

Supported data sources with QuickSight

Let's look at the different types of data sources that can be configured in Amazon QuickSight. A very common scenario for BI tools is to drive the visualizations from an analytical database or a data warehouse. Specifically, QuickSight supports the following **data warehouses**:

- Redshift with autodiscover

- Redshift manual connect

- Snowflake

- Teradata

> **Note**
>
> A use case for Redshift manual connect is when QuickSight and the Redshift cluster are in different AWS Regions.

Other **relational database systems** that are supported include the following:

- RDS

- MySQL

- PostgreSQL

- Oracle

- Amazon Aurora

- MariaDB

QuickSight also supports the following:

- Amazon Timestream

- Amazon Elasticsearch Service

Both are popular data stores for **time series datasets**.

For certain use cases, users might need to work with **individual files**, for example a Microsoft Excel file (.xls). Amazon QuickSight supports files as data sources either via direct upload or via a manifest file that points to the S3 location of one or more files.

QuickSight also supports popular **big data technologies**; specifically, the following:

- Amazon Athena

- Presto

- Spark

Another category is data sources from **APIs** and popular SaaS applications; specifically, the following:

- Salesforce

- GitHub

- Twitter

- Jira

- ServiceNow

- Adobe Analytics

Finally, QuickSight supports **AWS IoT Analytics** to visualize **Internet of Things (IoT)** data and integration with **S3 Analytics** to visualize access patterns on your S3 buckets.

Now that we have seen the data source options, in the next section we will configure our first data source using the **autodiscover feature**.

Configuring our first data source

In this section, we will configure our first two data sources, connecting the architecture we built in *Chapter 1, Introducing the AWS Analytics Ecosystem*.

Before we set up the data source in QuickSight, we will need to ensure that QuickSight service has a network route to our Redshift cluster. Since we are using the default settings, our cluster is locked down by default. We can confirm this by opening its security group. A security group acts as a virtual firewall to control the inbound and outbound traffic. The default security group will not allow any inbound or outbound traffic, unless it is coming from itself (a **self-referencing security group**). Therefore, without any action, Amazon QuickSight won't have access to the Redshift cluster. To allow QuickSight to access our Redshift cluster we will need to edit the security group of the Redshift cluster and allow inbound traffic from the IP address range of Amazon QuickSight.

In the next section, we will provide a step-by-step guide for enabling QuickSight access to our Redshift cluster.

Enabling access to the Redshift cluster

Let's start:

1. First, let's get the security group of our Redshift cluster:

    ```
    %aws redshift  describe-clusters --cluster-identifier
    mycluster --region us-east-1
    ```

    The AWS CLI response will contain a lot of information about the cluster. The security group ID can be found under the VpcSecurityGroups key of the API response:

    ```
    "VpcSecurityGroups": [
                {
                        "Status": "active",
                        "VpcSecurityGroupId": "sg-xxxxxxx"
                }
            ]
    ```

    Alternatively, we can easily find this information from the Redshift console. Navigate to the Redshift console, select your Redshift cluster (**mycluster**) and then select the **Properties** tab. The security information is under **Network and security settings**, so expand this option.

Figure 3.1 – Redshift Network and security settings tab

2. Now that we have the VPC security group ID, let's check its content to verify that it doesn't allow inbound access to Amazon QuickSight. Click on the security group ID to open the EC2 console and observe its rules. In the EC2 console, click on the security group ID and then select the inbound rules. You should be able to see a self-referencing inbound rule, but nothing else. Amazon QuickSight isn't a member of this security group; therefore, access is not possible at this stage.

3. Now that we have verified the inbound rules, we will add inbound access to Amazon QuickSight. To do that select **Edit inbound rules** to add a new rule. Select **Redshift** from the drop-down menu as the rule type. For the source, we will need to add the QuickSight service IP address space. To find this, we will need to look up the AWS documentation at `https://docs.aws.amazon.com/quicksight/latest/user/regions.html` and find the IP address space for the Region we are working in. In our example, we are working with **N. Virginia**. The QuickSight IP address range for that Region is `52.23.63.224/27`. Add this IP range as the source. It is a good practice to add a description to this rule to help you remember the purpose of this configuration, for example, `QuickSight Access to Redshift`.

4. Verify the values are as following:

   - **Type**: `Redshift`
   - **Protocol**: `TCP`
   - **Port Range**: `5439`
   - **Source**: **Custom** – `52.23.63.224/27`
   - **Description**: *QuickSight Access to Redshift*

5. Once these values are verified, click **Save rules**.

Now that we have configured network access between QuickSight and Redshift, in the next section we will set up our first Redshift data source.

Setting up a Redshift data source

In this section, we will set up our Redshift data source. For this step, we will need to access Amazon QuickSight using the Author user we created during *Chapter 2, Introduction to Amazon QuickSight*:

1. First, log in to Amazon QuickSight as the **Author** user. Once logged in, navigate to **Datasets** in the left-hand side menu and select **New Dataset**.

2. In the next screen, you will see a list of the supported QuickSight data sources. Select **Redshift (Auto-discovered)**.

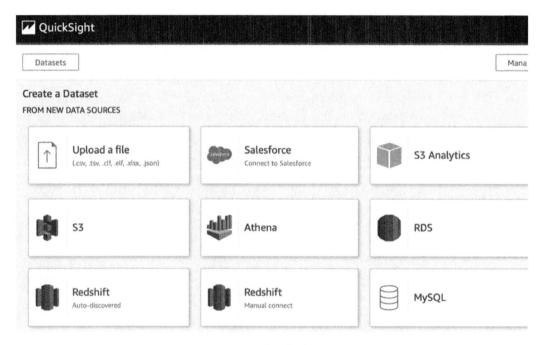

Figure 3.2 – QuickSight data sources

3. In the following screen, add the required information for the Redshift data source. You should be able to choose your cluster from the **Instance ID** drop-down menu.

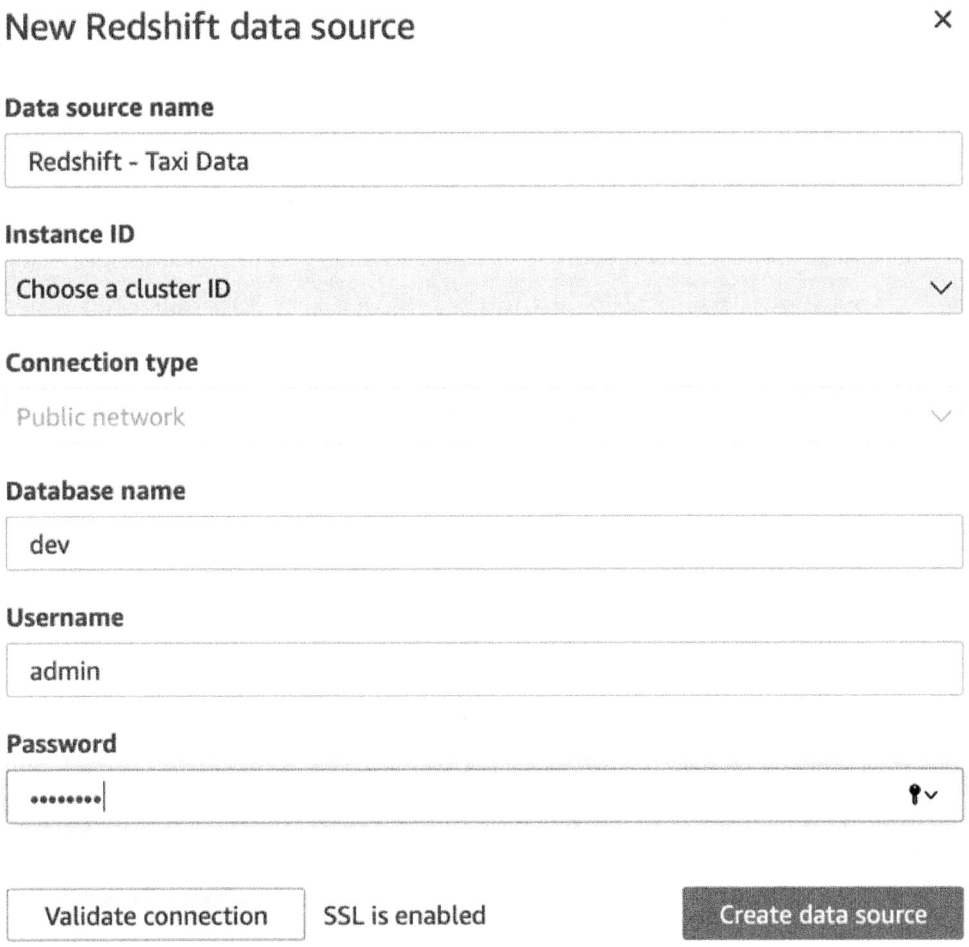

New Redshift data source   ✕

Data source name

Redshift - Taxi Data

Instance ID

Choose a cluster ID   ⌄

Connection type

Public network   ⌄

Database name

dev

Username

admin

Password

••••••••| 🔑⌄

Validate connection   SSL is enabled   Create data source

Figure 3.3 – Set up the Redshift data source

4. Once the form is completed, click **Create data source**.

Note

The **auto-discovered** option finds clusters in the same Region as QuickSight.
To verify the QuickSight Region or to change to the desired one, navigate to the
top right-hand corner of the screen and click on the drop-down icon next to
the username to reveal the Region settings.

---

5.   In the next screen, we will need to select the Redshift schema first. Once a schema is selected, we will see a list of tables for the selected schema.

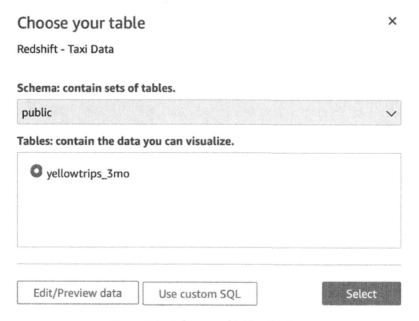

Figure 3.4 – Schema and table selection

Select **public** and then the **yellowtrips_3mo** table and click **Select**.

6.   Next, we will finalize the creation of the data source by selecting **Direct Query your data**.

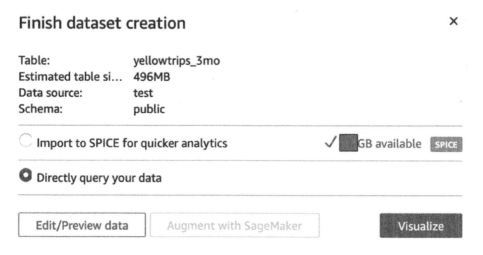

Figure 3.5 – Finalizing dataset creation

The last step will redirect you to the analysis web interface. We will work on this interface in *Chapter 4, Developing Visuals and Dashboards*. For now, click on the top left hand-side of the screen (the QuickSight logo) to go back to the QuickSight home page. You can verify the creation of the newly created dataset by accessing the dataset menu on the left-hand side.

To configure the Redshift Spectrum table, repeat the steps above. At the schema and table selection step, choose **spectrum_schema** (instead of **public**) and the **yellowtrips** table under that schema. Then repeat the steps as previous to configure a second Redshift data source for the Spectrum table we configured earlier. Note that the Redshift Spectrum tables aren't loaded into the data warehouse; instead, they reside in our data lake and they can be accessed and queried directly from there.

> **Note**
> To access the data into the Spectrum table, QuickSight will need to have access to the underlying data in Amazon S3.

Setting up an S3 data source

A common data source for QuickSight is S3. For example, you might want to visualize CSV files that are stored in Amazon S3. Before you configure an S3 data source, you need to ensure your QuickSight account has the required permissions to access the S3 locations where the files are stored.

> **Note**
> QuickSight doesn't automatically inherit access to newly created buckets. Even if you enable the **Access all buckets in my account** checkbox, QuickSight will only get access to every bucket in your account at that point in time, and not to any bucket you create from the point onward. If you need to add permissions to new buckets, you will need an AWS administrator to manage the permissions of the QuickSight service to AWS services in your account.

For the S3 data source, QuickSight requires a manifest file containing the required information to set up the datasets. The manifest file is in JSON format and contains the following objects:

- `fileLocations`: Here you will define the S3 location of the file (or files) you need to import by just appending the full S3 URI of your files (as a JSON array) using the `URIs` property. You can populate the `URIPrefixes` property, if you want to add all of the files that are under a specific S3 prefix (similar to a folder in a traditional filesystem).

- `globalUploadSettings`: The `globalUploadSettings` is optional. You can use this property to override the QuickSight default options. QuickSight will default to **CSV** format, using a "," (**comma**) field delimiter and **double quotes** (") as the text qualifier. By default, QuickSight will use the first row of the CSV file as the **header**, which implies that the first row will determine the dataset field names, and won't be considered as values in the dataset.

Now that we have learned how to configure certain datasets types, in the next section we will edit datasets using the QuickSight dataset editor.

Editing datasets

In this section, we will look more closely at the typical tasks an author user needs to do to edit a dataset. In real-world applications, it is common that datasets might need some degree of processing so that they can be used optimally by QuickSight.

These tasks include the following:

- Importing into SPICE
- Renaming fields
- Changing the field types
- Adding calculated fields
- Combining datasets together
- Applying security filters

In the next section, we will learn how to complete these tasks using the example dataset we configured earlier.

Importing into SPICE

It's time for us to learn how to import a dataset into SPICE. We will change the query mode using the dataset editor and then we will observe the status of the import job. Finally, we will learn how to schedule automatic refresh jobs for our SPICE datasets.

Setting the dataset query mode

Earlier in this chapter, we configured a Redshift dataset as a Direct Query. Let's assume that we realized that our data warehouse is busy serving many applications and producing reports for the organization, so we would prefer to import the data into SPICE, so that the QuickSight dashboards are using the SPICE storage, rather than accessing the data warehouse directly. After importing the data into SPICE, our data warehouse will only be used for data imports, and not for querying the data to populate the dashboards.

Now let's add our dataset into SPICE and configure its import duration:

1. First, you will need to log in as the author user we created earlier.

2. Then, select datasets on the left-hand side menu to get a list of all the datasets.

3. For this hands-on example, we will import the `yellowtrips_3mo` dataset into SPICE. Click on **yellowtrips_3mo** and then click **Edit dataset** on the pop-up window you see in the following screenshot.

Figure 3.6 – Dataset pop-up screen

4. Now we should be at the dataset editor main page. On this page, we will complete most of the operations to edit and transform our datasets later in this section. For now, we will just set **Query mode** to **SPICE** as shown in the following screenshot. Once done, click **Save**.

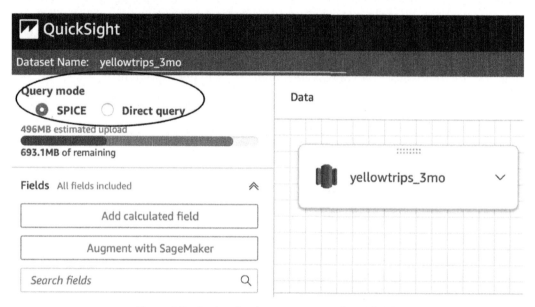

Figure 3.7 – Setting the dataset query mode to SPICE

5. You will notice that our dataset is now marked as a SPICE dataset. Now that we have set up the SPICE dataset for the first time, QuickSight will automatically run its first import job in the background.

Name		Owner	Last Modified ⌄
🗄 yellowtrips_3mo	SPICE	Me	a few seconds ago
🗄 yellowtrips		Me	7 days ago

Figure 3.8 – Viewing the SPICE datasets

Monitoring the import jobs status

After a few minutes, QuickSight will complete its first import job into SPICE. Next, we will gather information about the status of the import jobs:

1. First, click on the dataset name to get information about the import status, as shown in the following screenshot:

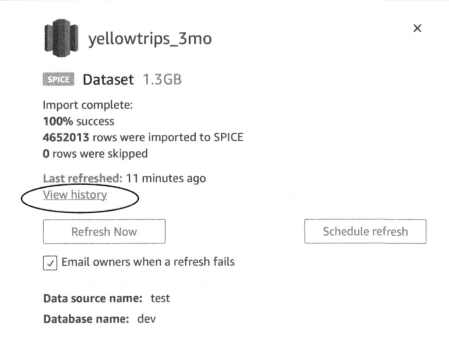

Figure 3.9 – View import status

From the first page we can observe that 4.6 million rows were imported successfully, using 1.3 GB of SPICE capacity.

2. Next, let's look at the history of the import. We can do that by simply clicking **View history**, and we will get a pop-up screen like the following:

View refresh history of yellowtrips_3mo

Figure 3.10 – View import history

3.   From the preceding screen we can get useful information about when the dataset was imported, how much time was required to import the dataset, the number of rows imported, and the number of rows skipped.

Now that we have covered the refresh and import jobs, in the next section we will look at how to automatically refresh the dataset.

Scheduling automatic refresh

QuickSight supports a simple refresh feature to automatically refresh datasets from SPICE. Specifically, users can set up hourly, daily, weekly, or monthly refresh jobs. Let's see how this is done:

> **Note**
>
> You can configure more than one refresh schedule for each dataset, unless your schedule is hourly. You can have up to one hourly refresh schedule per dataset.

1.   In our example, first you need to access the dataset and then click **Schedule refresh**, as shown in the following screenshot.

Figure 3.11 – Schedule refresh option

2.   Next, you will get a notification that there is no schedule, and you have the option to create a new schedule. Click on the **Create** button to create a new refresh schedule.

3.   Next, you can create your schedule using the editor shown in *Figure 3.12*. For the purposes of this tutorial, we don't need to create a scheduled refresh, as our dataset is static, but feel free to familiarize yourself with the various options.

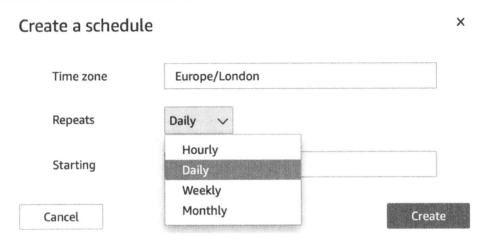

Figure 3.12 – The Create a schedule dialog

Now that we have learned how to configure SPICE datasets, schedule automatic refresh, and monitor the refresh jobs, in the next section we will learn how to edit datasets by renaming columns and data types.

Editing column names and data types

It is common for BI developers to edit their datasets before building visualizations. For example, a column name might not be as user friendly or as descriptive when it comes directly from a database. When designing BI applications, we need to think from the end-user perspective, and try to name the columns in a friendly and descriptive way that will make sense in the context of a BI application. Also, it is important to ensure that each field in our dataset has the expected data type, so that we can perform the required calculations. In this section, we will provide a step-by-step guide to edit our columns and data types using our SPICE dataset we configured earlier.

Renaming columns

Renaming columns using the dataset editor is a straightforward process:

1. First, we start by accessing the dataset and select the **Edit dataset** option, which will take us to the dataset editor page.

2. In the dataset editor, we can see a preview of our data including the column names, as shown in the following screenshot.

Figure 3.13 – Dataset preview screen

3. Next, we can simply rename the column names by clicking the pencil icon next to the column name. For example, let's rename the `tpep_pickup_datetime` column to the user-friendlier name of `Pick up date` as shown in the next screenshot. At this stage, we can also give a column description to describe the column to other authors who might work on the same dataset.

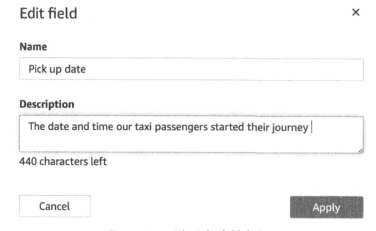

Figure 3.14 – The Edit field dialog

Now that we have seen how to edit a column name and description, in the next section we will see how to edit data types.

Changing data types

By using the right data type for every column, we can make sure to access the right functionality for each column in our datasets. For example, QuickSight supports time aggregation for date column types. If a date column is incorrectly mapped as a string column, then those aggregations cannot be used. Similarly, calculations such as calculating the average or min/max applies only to numerical data types. If we need to perform and visualize these calculations, we will need to ensure that a numerical data type has been applied.

QuickSight supports the following data types:

- String
- Date
- Decimal
- Integer

The following geospatial types are also supported:

- County
- State
- City
- Postcod
- Latitude
- Longitude

Now, let's see a quick hands-on example of how to edit data types in our dataset. For this example, we will use the `yellowtrips` dataset (in the `yellowtrips_3mo` set, the column data types seem to be correct, so there is nothing to edit).

1. First, we will need to access the `yellowtrips` dataset and navigate to the dataset editor.

2. In this dataset, you can see that the date columns have been identified as strings. This is something that we will need to edit, so that we can use time-based aggregations later on in our analysis.

3. To change the data type, we will need to click on the data type (**String** in this example) under the column name and select **Date**.

4. Next, QuickSight will open the edit date format pop-up screen as shown in the following screenshot. We will need to define the date format of our dataset. In our example, this is yyyy-MM-dd HH:mm:ss, where yyyy represents the year using four digits (for example, 2020); MM the month using two digits (such as 02 for February), and so on similarly for the other elements in this syntax. Once we enter the date format, QuickSight will validate our dataset against the date format chosen to ensure that the data complies with it.

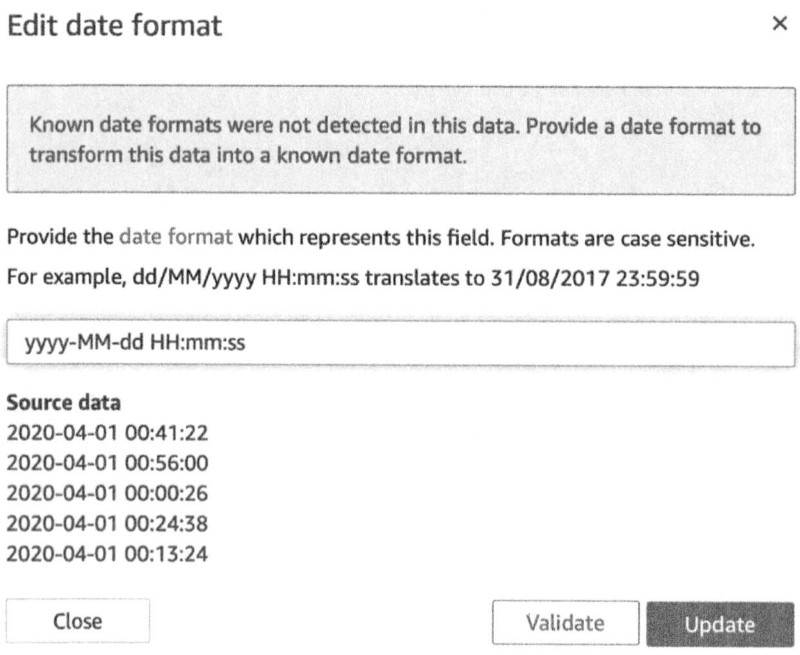

Edit date format   ×

> Known date formats were not detected in this data. Provide a date format to transform this data into a known date format.

Provide the date format which represents this field. Formats are case sensitive.

For example, dd/MM/yyyy HH:mm:ss translates to 31/08/2017 23:59:59

    yyyy-MM-dd HH:mm:ss

Source data
2020-04-01 00:41:22
2020-04-01 00:56:00
2020-04-01 00:00:26
2020-04-01 00:24:38
2020-04-01 00:13:24

    Close   Validate   Update

Figure 3.15 – Edit date format

We can repeat the process for the tpep_dropoff_datetime column. Now that we have learned how to edit columns, including changing column names and types and adding descriptions, in the next section we will learn advanced dataset operations including joins and security controls.

Working with advanced operations

In this section, we will focus on advanced dataset operations. We will learn to add calculated fields to our dataset and apply dataset operations such as filtering and joining. Finally, we will add security controls, including row- and column-level filters. For this section, we will use our SPICE dataset that we configured earlier in this chapter.

Adding calculated fields

QuickSight allows BI developers to add calculated fields to their datasets at the data preparation stage. This dataset, including its calculated fields, can then be used to develop multiple analyses.

There are a number of prebuilt functions with QuickSight that we can use when building a calculated field. Those functions include the following:

- **Aggregate functions** are used to calculate metrics over a number of values. For example, we can use the `min()` function to calculate the minimum value of a set of values.

- **Conditional functions** allow us to use conditional logic in a calculated field, for example, `isNotNull()` returns `true` if the argument passed is not null.

- **Date functions** help us work with date column types. For example, we can use the `dateDiff()` function to calculate the difference between two date fields.

- **Numeric functions** and **string functions** can help us work with numerical values and string values respectively. For example, we can calculate the absolute value of a given expression using the `abs()` function or we can concatenate two or more strings using the `concat()` function.

- Finally, **table calculations**, can be used to discover how dimensions influence specific measures. For example, the `sumOver()` function calculates the sum of a measure partitioned by a list of dimensions.

To add a calculated field, we do the following:

1. First, we need to open our dataset in the dataset editor.

2. Then, we can simply select the **Add calculated field** option to get to the calculated field editor, as shown here:

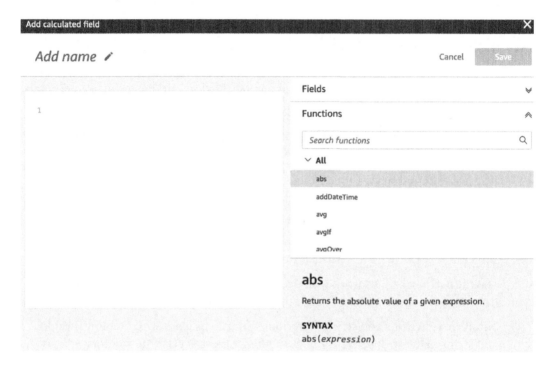

Figure 3.16 – Calculated field editor

3. Next, let's add our first calculated field. In our dataset, while we have the pick-up time and drop-off time, it might be interesting to get the difference between these two timestamps in minutes. To calculate this, we can type the following:

```
dateDiff({Pick up Date},{tpep_dropoff_datetime},"MI")
```

4. Finally, let's give a descriptive name, for example `Trip duration(mins)`, and click **Save**.

Now we can observe our new calculated field in the dataset editor. Next, we will see other dataset operations including filtering and joining.

Filtering and joining datasets

In this section, we will discuss how to filter and join data sources together.

Filtering datasets

There are scenarios where you might need a subset of the table from a data source. QuickSight supports data source filtering so you can import the required subset of a dataset into SPICE. That allows you to build efficient BI solutions by only using the SPICE capacity that's really required. Adding a filter in QuickSight is simple. In the following example, we will see an example of how to filter out columns and rows from the dataset we created earlier:

1. First, you will need to access the dataset editor. On the left-hand side, you can find the **Excluded fields** and **Filters** menus.

2. For this example, let's assume that we aren't interested in the information in the store_and_fwd_flag column. To exclude this column from our dataset, expand the **Excluded fields** option and then select **store_and_fwd_flag**.

3. Now that we have removed a column, let's apply a filter to remove rows. Let's assume that for this analysis, we don't want to include trips if the distance is shown as 0.0, and we only want data where the value is greater than 0.

4. Expand the **Filter** menu and select the trip_distance column. Select **Greater than** from the drop-down menu and then **0**. After adding those values, the filter should look as in the following screenshot:

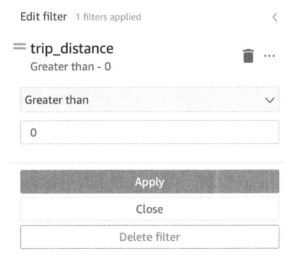

Figure 3.17 – Adding dataset filters

5. Next, click **Apply**. QuickSight will trigger a refresh job for the dataset.

Now that we have learned how to apply filters on datasets, in the next section, we will enrich our dataset by joining it with reference data.

Joining datasets

Joining datasets can be used to combine datasets together and provide a single view of our data. Having relevant and good-quality data is key to the success of our BI application. For this example, we will enrich the dataset we used earlier with a reference dataset that can be downloaded from the website provider. Alternatively, we can create a lookup CSV file and upload it to QuickSight. Let's begin:

1. First, let's download our small lookup table from `https://s3.amazonaws.com/nyc-tlc/misc/taxi+_zone_lookup.csv`.

2. Next, on the dataset editor, click **Add data** and then upload the file.

3. Upload the lookup file.

4. Next, select the location ID for the join column and select **Left** as the join configuration. See the following screenshot for an example.

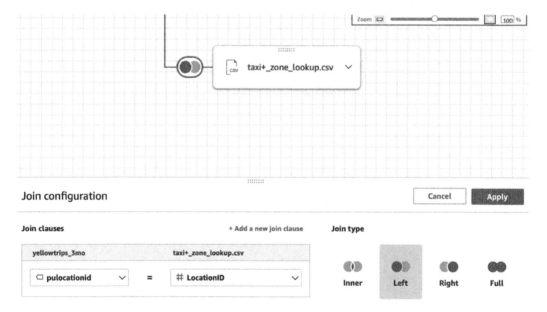

Figure 3.18 – Join configurations

5. Once applied, you can confirm the new columns in the dataset editor.

Now that we have learned how to join datasets, we will learn how to add security controls to our datasets.

Configuring security controls

QuickSight supports row-level and column-level security controls. In this section, we will learn how to add security controls to our datasets.

Adding column-level security controls

In certain cases, BI developers might want to restrict access to specific columns to protect sensitive data (such as personally identifiable data). Once a BI developer adds column-level security, only the allowed users will be able to view and access the restricted column. By default, when you share a dataset with another user, you give them access to all columns of this dataset. Therefore, you will need to add column-level security controls if you need to restrict certain columns. To add column-level security, you can select the **Column-level security** option.

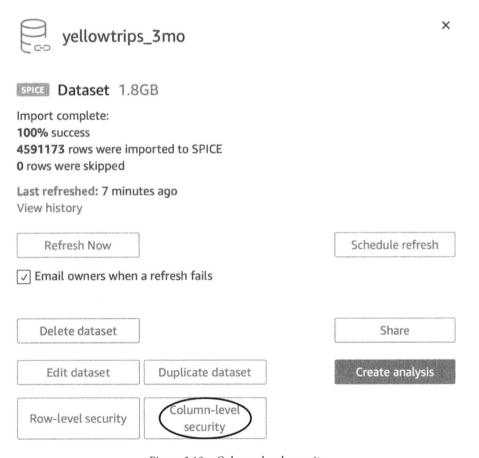

Figure 3.19 – Column-level security

You will then see the list of columns in your dataset. You will notice that by default, users and groups with access to the dataset have access to all columns. To restrict a column, you will need to select it and then add the users or groups you want to enable access for. This selection will override the "everyone" default setting and only the users or groups you add will have access. Once completed, you will notice a padlock icon next to your dataset to confirm that security restrictions are present.

Adding row-level security

QuickSight supports row-level security for your datasets. Row filters are particularly useful when you want certain users or groups to have different levels of access to a subset of data depending on their username or group membership. To apply row-level security you will need to provide a permissions file or create a permissions table in your database and then add it to QuickSight. In our example, the vendorid column has two distinct values, 2 and 1, each representing a different vendor. Let's imagine a scenario where users from vendor 1 need to have access to the dataset, but they should only be able to access the vendor 1 data and not data from vendor 2. Likewise, vendor 2 should only be allowed to view their data. For this example, we can apply row-based security controls.

Applying a row-level filter

For our example, we can consider two different users, user1 for vendor 1 and user2 for vendor 2. QuickSight will match the username accessing the dataset with the value of the UserName field and then apply the filter or filters using the remaining column. In our example, it will use the vendorid column from the yellowtrips_3mo dataset.

See our following mapping table for the scenario described previously:

UserName	vendorid
user1	1
user2	2

Figure 3.20 – Mapping table

To apply row-based permissions, we need to do the following:

1. We save the mapping table as a `.csv` file and then import it as a new dataset. The format of the file will be as follows:

    ```
    UserName,vendorid
    user1,"1"
    user2,"2"
    <your-admin-user>,""
    ```

2. Edit the newly created dataset, and ensure that `vendorid` field is of type **String**.

3. Then, select the **yellowtrips_3mo** dataset and select **Row-level security,** as shown in the following screenshot:

Figure 3.21 – Add row-level security

4. Then select the mapping table you added in *step 1*.

5. Then click on **Apply to dataset**. Now the filter has been applied, as shown in the following screenshot:

Configure row-level security

yellowtrips_3mo

Selected dataset rules

mapping-table-new

Figure 3.22 – Dataset rules applied

We will not need these permissions for the next chapter. After you have applied the row-level filters, you can remove them by doing the following:

1. Select the **yellowtrips_3mo** dataset and then **Row-level security.**
2. With the mapping table selected, click on **Remove dataset.**
3. Click **Remove dataset** again to confirm the action.

Summary

Congratulations on completing this chapter. In this chapter, we learned how to create and edit datasets in Amazon QuickSight. We managed to import datasets into SPICE and schedule automatic refresh jobs. We also edited fields and added custom calculations to get more value from a dataset and its columns. We then looked at advanced dataset operations including joining datasets together and enriching them with reference data. In the last part of this chapter, we learned how to apply security controls, either at the column level or row level, so that you can protect sensitive information or apply specific filters to your users.

In the next chapter, we will learn how to visualize datasets with QuickSight analyses and dashboards.

Q&A

1. What is the difference between a direct query and a SPICE data source?
2. How do you add column-level security controls in Amazon QuickSight?
3. When might we need row-level security for our dataset?
4. Why might we need to exclude columns from a dataset?
5. How do we enrich a dataset with reference data?
6. Why is it important to configure the correct data type for every column in our dataset?

Further reading

- *QuickSight User Guide – Preparing data*: `https://docs.aws.amazon.com/quicksight/latest/user/preparing-data.html`

4
Developing Visuals and Dashboards

In this chapter, we will introduce the main analysis building functionality of Amazon QuickSight. We will start by exploring the author user interface and understanding the different visual types. After adding certain visual types and explaining their functionality, we will introduce the concept of a dashboard and show how to share dashboards with business users with simple, hands-on examples. Finally, we will look at how to style a dashboard using existing or custom themes.

In this chapter, we will cover the following topics:

- Working with QuickSight visuals
- Publishing dashboards
- Customizing the look and feel of the application

Technical requirements

For this chapter, you will need the following:

- An AWS account
- A QuickSight account with the author and reader users configured
- The datasets we created in *Chapter 3, Preparing Data with Amazon QuickSight*

Working with QuickSight visuals

Visuals are defined as the on-screen widgets that you can add to your QuickSight analysis to visualize your data. Selecting the right visual type is important for the success of your BI application. In this section, we will learn about the supported visual types and how to select the most appropriate visual type for different scenarios.

Creating an analysis

Before we look at the available visual types, we need to create our first analysis. QuickSight analysis is the main user interface for developing your BI applications. While working on an analysis, you will be able to add data visualization widgets, configure ML capabilities, and configure the look and feel of your BI application.

To create an analysis, perform the following steps:

1. First, log into QuickSight as an author user.

2. Next, select **Analyses** from the left-hand side menu and select **New analysis**, as shown in the following screenshot:

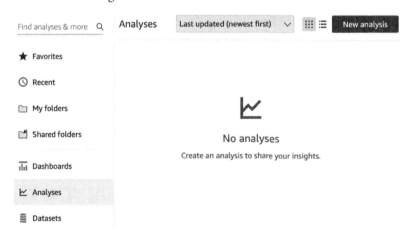

Figure 4.1 – Analyses menu

3. You will then need to select a dataset to start your analysis. Choose the yellowtrips_3mo dataset we configured earlier and select **Create Analysis**.

4. This will take you to the main analysis user interface, as shown in the following screenshot:

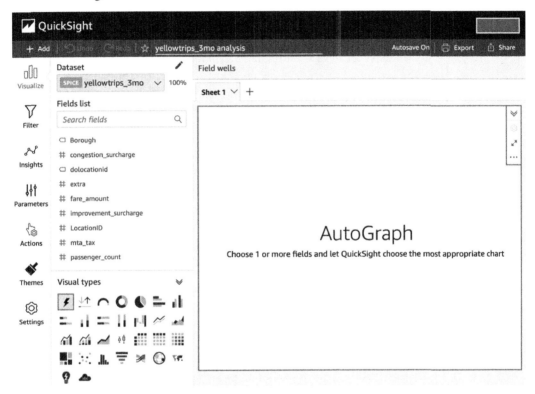

Figure 4.2 – Analysis user interface

This is the main user interface that we will be using throughout this book to develop our BI application.

> **Note**
>
> Familiarize yourself with the analysis user interface, including the main screen, the top menu, the side menu, the field wells, the dataset, the column list, and the visual types selection tool as we will be using them throughout this book.

Next, we will focus on the different visual types by looking at examples using our example datasets.

Supported visual types

QuickSight supports several visual types that you can choose to visualize your data with. AWS is constantly expanding this list. In the next few sections, we will explore those types by focusing on the business question and how the visuals can help you address them.

Visualizing a metric or a key performance indicator

There are scenarios where you might want to visualize a **key performance indicator** (**KPI**). Visualizing the progress of a metric against a target metric or comparing the monthly sales of the current month with the sales of the last month are examples of KPIs that organizations often need to monitor. The two visual types that are ideal for these types of visualizations are as follows:

- **KPI visual type**
- **Gauge chart**

Let's look closer at each of these visual types using the dataset we created in *Chapter 3, Preparing Data with Amazon QuickSight*.

The KPI visual type

The **KPI visual type** allows you to display metrics, including comparisons against time intervals or a trend. To select the KPI visual type, you simply need to select the ⬆ icon. Then, you can start parameterizing your KPI visual, as shown in the following screenshot:

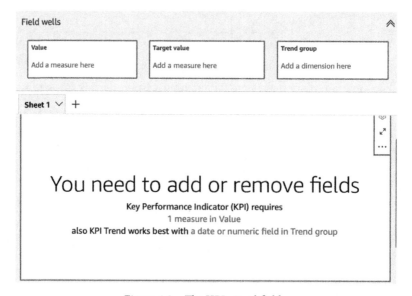

Figure 4.3 – The KPI visual fields

The KPI visual allows us to set up three types of fields:

- **Value**: This field represents the value we want to measure.

- **Target value**: This field represents the target metric we want to compare the value field against.

- **Trend group**: There are scenarios where you will need to visualize how a metric is trending; for example, a trend over time. The trend group field can be used for this purpose.

> **Note**
>
> You can use either a target value or a trend group with the KPI visual, but not both.

To understand the KPI visual, we will look at an example of using the New York Taxi dataset we imported into QuickSight earlier in this book. For this example, let's assume we want to visualize how the tips are performing compared to the overall fare. A tip value below 10% of the total might indicate that people aren't very generous with their tips. Let's see what the data tells us!

For this KPI visual, we will use `tip_amount` as the value field and `total_amount` as the target. To add these fields, simply drag and drop each field to the corresponding column, as shown here. Once you've added these fields, the visual should look as follows:

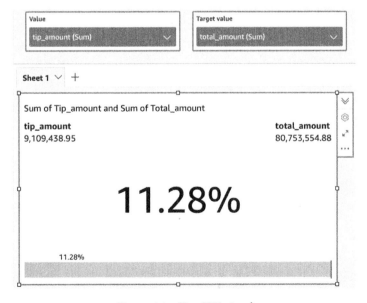

Figure 4.4 – Tips KPI visual

Now that we have our first KPI visual, we will configure some of its parameters. Each field that's in a field can be configured individually by selecting the respective drop-down menu, as follows:

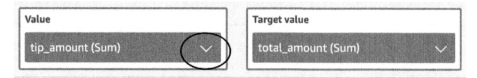

Figure 4.5 – Field options

From this menu, we can choose how the field is aggregated and how it is formatted. For aggregation, we have the following options:

- **Sum** (default).
- **Average**.
- **Count**.
- **Count distinct**.
- **Max**.
- **Median**.
- **Min**.
- **Percentile**: When percentile is selected, you will also need to select the percentile value; for example, 95 to calculate P95.
- **Standard deviation**.
- **Standard deviation**: Population.
- **Variance**.
- **Variance**: Population.

For our example, we can keep the default setting, which is the **Sum** aggregation, as it shows us the total amount of tips and fares. Next, let's look at the format. The available options are as follows:

- **Number**
- **Currency**
- **Percentage**

The **Currency** format type fits better for our field. Once the type has been selected, you will be able to edit the format in detail by selecting the **More formatting options** menu. Finally, we can format the entire visual by selecting the cog icon next to our visual. This will open up a menu where we can edit the comparison format (for example, the percentage of actual values), change the font size, and change the title. Let's set the title to **New York Taxi Tips Percentage** and set the subtitle to **10% Target**. Now, the visual should look as follows:

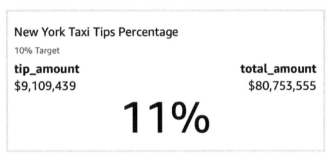

Figure 4.6 – New York Taxi Tips Percentage KPI

Now that we have seen how to configure the KPI visual type, we will learn how to configure the gauge chart visual.

The gauge chart

The gauge chart is a useful way to compare a value with the target value. Gauge charts help us visualize the progress against a target.

> Note
>
> A similar visualization to the gauge chart can be achieved with the progress bar on the KPI visual.

To understand the gauge chart, we can use our New York Taxi dataset. For this example, let's assume that our target for these 3 months is to have 6.5 million passengers and we want to compare the actual numbers against this target. A quick way to add this target value is to simply create a calculated field and assign it with the value 6,500,000. This value will be added to every row of our dataset, increasing the total SPICE space required. Then, we can use `passenger_count (sum)` as the **Value** field of the gauge chart and the newly created calculated field (aggregated as the average) as the **Target** field. Similar to the KPI chart that we saw earlier, we will be able to access additional settings for this visual, such as setting a title, controlling the values that are displayed, the thickness of the fonts, the data labels, and the tooltip. Feel free to get familiar with the settings of this visual. With the default settings (and only increased font size) the gauge visual will look as follows:

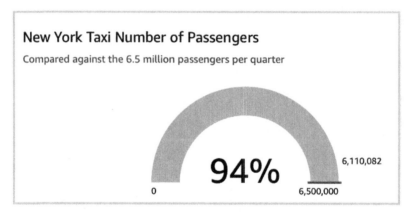

Figure 4.7 – The gauge chart

Now that we have learned how to visualize KPIs, we can focus on other visual types. Next, we will look at using visual types to help us visualize the composition of a selected attribute in our dataset.

Visualizing the composition of an attribute

Visualizing the composition of one or more of your dataset dimensions can be a common question you want to answer with your BI application. For example, you might want to see how much each region contributes to the total sales. In our example, we can visualize how much each taxi zone contributes to the total taxi fares collected. These types of questions can be visualized with the following types of charts:

- **Pie charts**
- **Donut charts**

When setting up both visuals, you will need to specify a group/color field and the value field.

> **Note**
>
> If you don't specify a value field, QuickSight will default to the count of records.

Using our example dataset, we will use a donut chart to visualize the records by service zone. Similarly, we will use a pie chart to visualize the count of records by borough. For this purpose, we can set the `service_zone` field and then the `Borough` field as a group/color for the donut chart and the pie chart, respectively. As a result, the two visuals will look as follows:

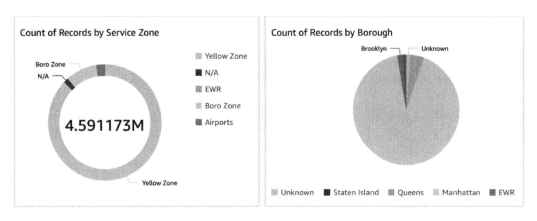

Figure 4.8 – The donut and pie charts

Both visual types can help you visualize the composition of an attribute, and they work particularly well when you have a small number of categories. Both visual types are not very effective when you want to do side-by-side comparisons. Next, we will look at visual types that can help you visualize such side-by-side comparisons.

Visualizing side-by-side comparisons

QuickSight allows you to visualize side-by-side comparisons by offering several bar chart options. Horizontal, vertical, or stacked bar charts are some examples of this type of visual. To understand these visuals, we will use our dataset and configure a bar chart. Let's assume we want to understand and compare the tip percentage for each of the New York boroughs:

1. First, we need a calculated field and must assign the `{tip_amount}/{fare_amount}` value to Tip Percentage.

2. Next, we will need to add our visual. A bar chart would be an ideal solution to compare the tip percentage for each borough.

A bar chart, either vertical or horizontal, will need the following fields to be configured:

- **X axis**

- **Value**

- (Optionally) **Group/color**

The *x* axis is the primary dimension that you want to understand for your value. In our example, this will be the `Borough` field. For the value field, you will need to set the value you want to understand and compare. In our example, this will be the newly created `Tip Percentage` calculated field, aggregated as the average. Finally, you can add a `Group/Color` field, if you need to add another dimension to your visual.

> **Note**
> A bar chart needs at least an x-axis and a value field. The group/color field is optional. You can set more than one value field if you need to monitor multiple values in the same visual.

Once we've applied these fields, this is what the vertical bar chart will look like:

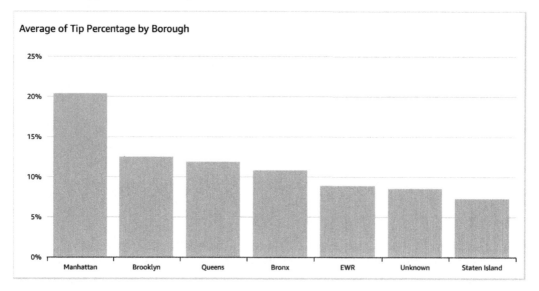

Figure 4.9 – Vertical bar chart

Now that we have learned how to use a simple bar chart, in the next section, we will learn how to visualize time series.

Visualizing time series

It is common for BI applications to visualize how a metric is changing over time. Time series data is usually represented with line charts. Time series visualizations need to ensure that temporal fields are stored as the Date field type in QuickSight. This will enable time-based aggregations; for example, day, week, month, quarter, or year.

In this section, we will use a simple line chart to create our first time series visualization. Let's assume that we want to visualize the total amount of taxi fares over time so that we can observe how the fare amount is distributed over time.

A line chart requires you to define the following:

- **X axis**: In time series, this will be our temporal field.
- **Value**: The value you want to measure over time.
- Optionally, the **Color** field: When you want to visualize multiple categories, you can use the Color field. This will result in multiple lines on the same line chart.

For our example, you will need to pick tpep_dropoff_datetime as the x-axis and total_amount (Sum) as the value. This dataset is only for 3 months; therefore, a daily aggregate is likely to have enough data points for a meaningful data visualization. You will need to ensure that the daily aggregation is chosen. To do that, select the x-axis column and expand the drop-down menu, as shown in the following screenshot:

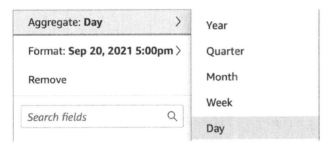

Figure 4.10 – Time-based aggregations

The following screenshot shows a line chart of the total fare amount aggregated daily for the period from September to December:

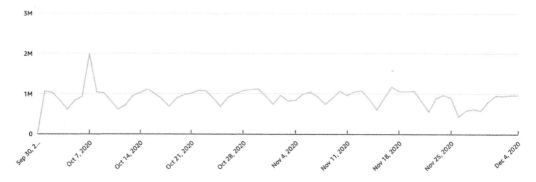

Figure 4.11 – The line chart

Now that we have learned how to set up line charts, we will learn how to use table visuals.

Using tables

Tables can be useful when we want to display the values of specific metrics, without using other visual means. Table visuals can be used to display raw data, which can be useful for users familiar with the data being used to populate a BI application. QuickSight supports the following:

- **Table visual** for simple table visualizations
- **Pivot table** visual for tables that need to summarize data in multiple dimensions

For the simple **table visual**, you will need to define the **value** and the **group by** fields in the field well. The *group by* field is used to aggregate your data, while the *value* field contains the metrics that will be added to the table, broken down by the **group by** fields. You can add one or more **value** fields if you are interested in more than one metric. You can use one or more **group by** fields; however, a pivot table might be a better fit if you need to break down the data using more than one dimension.

To understand the use of tables, let's use our example dataset. For this example, let's assume that we want to visualize a table with the total fare amount broken down by borough. For this visual, we will use the `Borough` column as the group by field and `fare_amount (sum)` as the value field.

You can customize a table visual with additional options. First, you can control the visual title and column names. In our example, we can replace the `fare_amount` column name with the user-friendly name *Fare amount*, which is easier to read. Additionally, we can choose to display a total aggregate of the value fields and control how and where the total will be displayed. In our example, the total will be useful to add to the table.

> **Note**
>
> The total is not shown by default in the table visual, so we will need to enable it if we need to show it.

Feel free to familiarize yourself with the additional settings by accessing the cog icon on the right-hand side of the visual. In the following screenshot, you can see a table visual using our sample data:

Taxi fares by borough

Borough	Fare Amount
Total	$55,791,387
Bronx	$1,122,186
Brooklyn	$2,172,315
EWR	$2,907
Manhattan	$45,001,178
Queens	$6,022,819
Staten Island	$77,035
Unknown	$1,392,948

Figure 4.12 – The table visual

Now, let's assume that we want to provide a table to our readers that allows them to dive deeper into each borough's data and break it down by payment type. A pivot table visual can be used instead of a simple table. In pivot tables, you can define the following:

- **Rows**
- **Columns**
- **Values** as rows or as columns

In our example, we will use the `fare_amount` column as the value field (as a column). For the row fields, we will add two fields this time: `Borough` and `Payment Type`. Similar to the table visual, you can use the cog icon to access the additional settings to change your visual's title, field naming, and total calculation. Additionally, pivot tables can display subtotals for each category and have additional styling controls. The following pivot table is using the dataset from our example:

Fare amounts by borough and payment type

Borough	Payment Type	fare_amount
⊟ Bronx	null	$969,806.58
	Cash	$50,961.67
	Credit Card	$100,715.51
	Dispute	-$334.70
	No Charge	$1,036.51
	Subtotal	$1,122,185.57
⊞ Brooklyn		$2,172,314.53
⊞ EWR		$2,907.37
⊞ Manhattan		$45,001,178....
⊞ Queens		$6,022,818.58
⊞ Staten Island		$77,034.66
⊞ Unknown		$1,392,948.05

Figure 4.13 – The pivot table visual

Now that we have learned how to use tables, in the next section, we will learn about visualizing geospatial data.

Visualizing geospatial data

QuickSight can work with geospatial data. At the time of writing, QuickSight supports two types of geospatial visuals:

- **Points on map**
- **Filled map**

The **points on map** visual is a good fit when you need to highlight specific points on the map. The size of the point is determined from the `Size` field. When you need to visualize different categories, you can add multiple colors. The points on map visual works well with coordinates, but it can work with other geospatial data types too, such as city, state, and country.

The **filled map** visual might be a better fit when you need to visualize a metric that covers wider geography, such as a country. When creating a filled map visual, you will need to define two fields: the location field and the color field.

In the next section, we will learn how to visualize the flow between the source and a destination.

Visualizing the flow between the source and a destination

There are scenarios where you might want to visualize a metric while considering a source and a destination. The **Sankey** visual type can be a great fit when we need to visualize a metric that flows between a source and a destination. The Sankey diagram depicts the flow from the source to a destination as a line. The width of the line depends on the value of the metric. For example, in our dataset, we capture the taxi pick-up and drop-off locations. We can enrich the location ID using a lookup table and get the pick-up borough and drop-off borough. Now, let's assume that we want to visualize the total miles traveled between the New York boroughs. Using the Sankey visual type, we will need to set `Pick Up Borough` as the `Source` field, `Drop off Borough` as the `Destination` field, and `trip_distance` as the `Weigh` field.

The following screenshot shows an example Sankey visual using our example dataset:

Figure 4.15 – The Sankey visual type

Now that we have learned how to work with most of the visual types that are available, in the next section, we will learn how to publish our analysis so that it can be shared with other users.

Publishing dashboards

In this section, we will learn how to publish a dashboard and share it with other reader users. A dashboard is the read-only version of an analysis that can be consumed by reader users. A dashboard is not a point-in-time snapshot of the analysis. When a user accesses a dashboard, QuickSight will fetch the data to populate the dashboard visuals. Depending on how you configured your data source, data is fetched either using a direct query or using **SPICE**. When you use SPICE data sources, QuickSight will scale automatically for the number of users you have. When you query your data source directly, you need to ensure that the data source (for example, a data warehouse) has enough resources to support the workload.

Sharing a dashboard is easy. Let's take a look:

1. First, you will need to open the analysis you want to share as a dashboard.

2. Click on the **Share** button on the top-right corner of the screen. This will open the **Publish a dashboard** screen, as shown in the following screenshot:

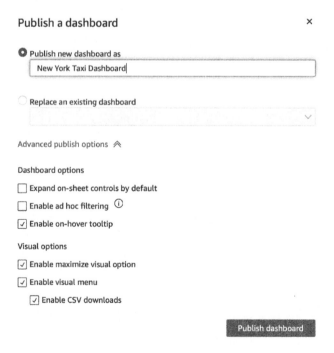

Figure 4.16 – Publish a dashboard screen

3. Type in a name – for example, `New York Taxi Dashboard` – and then click **Publish dashboard**.

4. After a few seconds, the dashboard will be generated and the **Share dashboard** screen will appear, as shown in the following screenshot:

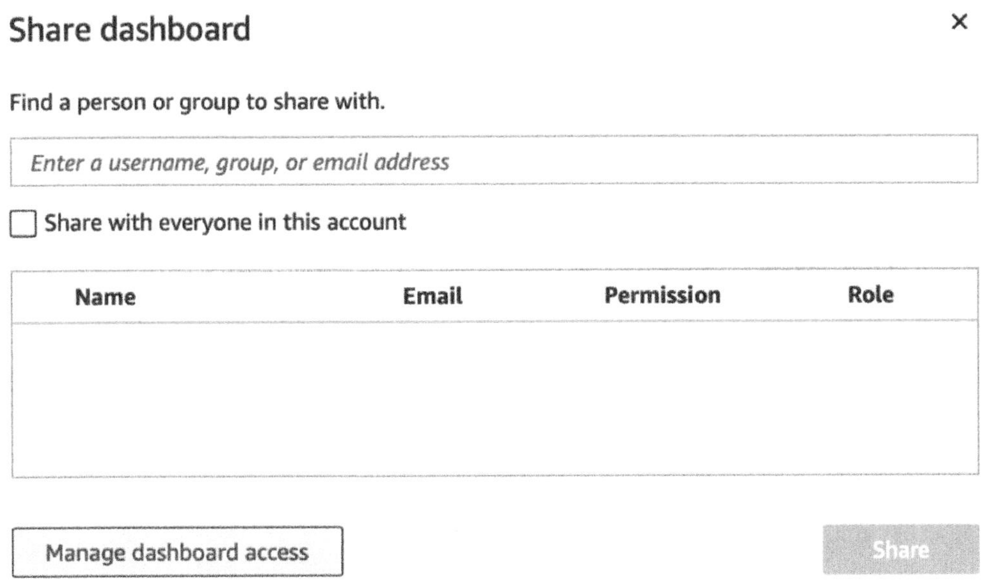

Share dashboard   ✕

Find a person or group to share with.

Enter a username, group, or email address

☐ Share with everyone in this account

Name	Email	Permission	Role

| Manage dashboard access | Share

Figure 4.17 – Share dashboard screen

5. Add any users or groups you want to share your dashboard with and click **Share**.

6. Congratulations – you have created your first QuickSight dashboard! This can be seen in the following screenshot:

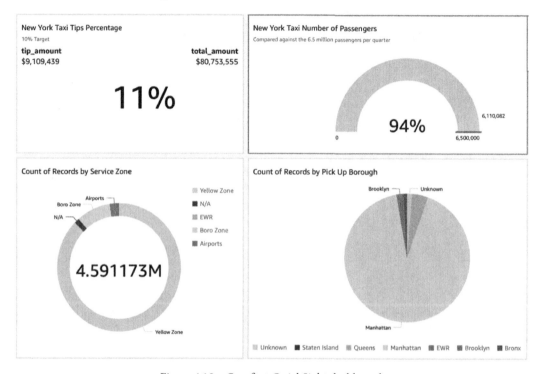

Figure 4.18 – Our first QuickSight dashboard

A QuickSight dashboard is primarily used by business users who want to get insights from the organization's data. For these users, the look and feel of the application can be an important factor. In the next section, we will learn about some of the basic controls we can use to change the look and feel of our BI application.

Customizing the look and feel of the application

In this section, we will focus on the look and feel of the application. There are different reasons why we might need to change the default look and feel of the application. For example, an organization might need to use colors that match its branding. In this section, we will learn how to do the following:

- Apply themes
- Format individual visuals

Let's get started!

Applying themes

Themes in QuickSight are a collection of look-and-feel settings that can be applied to multiple analyses and dashboards. To access the **Themes** menu, we will need to have an analysis open:

1. First, log in as an author user and open an analysis. Here, we will use the New York Taxi analysis that we have developed in this chapter.

2. Notice that on the left-hand side menu, the **Themes** option is present. Click on the **Themes** menu, as follows:

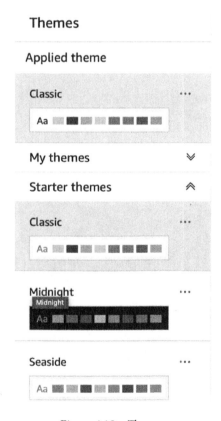

Figure 4.19 – Themes

3. Notice that there are prebuilt themes that we can start with. For this example, we will select the **Midnight** theme and observe the look and feel using the dashboard we created earlier.

4. Select the **Midnight** theme.

5. Now, we need to refresh our dashboard. Click on the **Share** option at the top right-hand side of the screen, and then click **Publish dashboard**.

6. This time, we will need to replace an existing dashboard, rather than create a new one. See the following example:

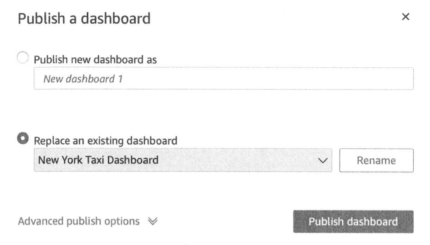

Figure 4.20 – Updating an existing dashboard

7. Observe the new look and feel of our dashboard, as shown in the following screenshot:

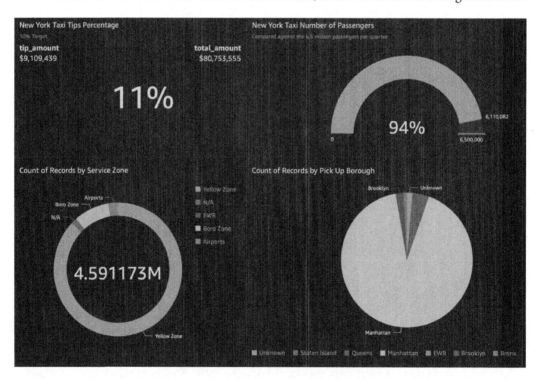

Figure 4.21 – Dashboard with the Midnight theme applied

> **Note**
>
> You can create a theme using your colors and a selection of different fonts. Consult the AWS documentation to understand how each color group setting is used by QuickSight.

While themes can be applied to all visuals of an analysis, you might want to change the colors of an individual visual. In the next section, we will learn how to change the look and feel of individual visuals.

Formatting visuals

You might want to change the color of a specific visual or change the color of a specific data point within a visual. In other cases, you might want to apply formatting settings based on specific conditions. In this section, you will learn how to do the following:

- Edit the colors of a specific visual.
- Apply conditional formatting.

Let's get started!

Editing the color of a specific visual

To edit the colors of a specific visual, follow these steps:

1. First, open an analysis and click on a colored area of your visual to open the color options, as shown in the following screenshot:

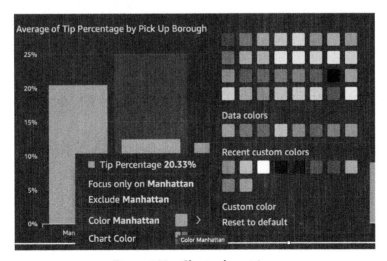

Figure 4.22 – Chart color settings

2. Notice that our bar chart has only one color. Let's assume that we want to change the chart color and that we also want the top value (Manhattan) to be highlighted with another color.

3. To change the color of the chart, you need to pick the color you want from the **Chart Color** options. You can select a set of predefined colors, or you can pick a custom color.

4. Finally, to change only the top value – *Manhattan*, in our example – you need to pick a color from **Color Manhattan**. You can choose from a set of predefined colors or pick a custom color.

5. The following screenshot shows the charts after making the color changes described in the previous steps:

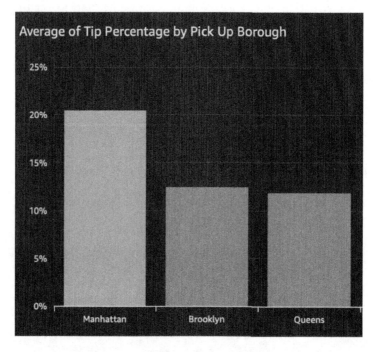

Figure 4.23 – Bar chart after updating its color

Now that we have learned how to change the color of a visual, let's learn how to apply conditional formatting.

Applying conditional formatting

Some visual types support conditional formatting. Conditional formatting can be used when you need to control the look and feel of your visual based on a condition. In this section, we will select one of the visuals we developed earlier and apply conditional formatting.

The gauge chart visual supports visual formatting. For this example, let's assume that we want the color of the text to be red when the percentage target is below 95%:

1. First, we will need to access the **Conditional formatting** settings, as shown in the following screenshot:

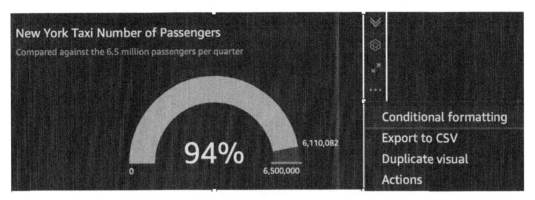

Figure 4.24 – Conditional formatting menu

2. In this example, we are interested in changing the text color, so we need to click the **Add text color** option.

3. Then, we must configure the condition, as follows:

    a) Format field based on: **Percent (%)**

    b) Condition: **Less than**

    c) Value (%): **95**

    d) Color: **Red**:

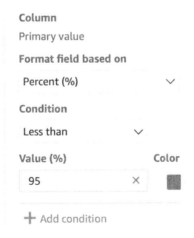

Figure 4.25 – Adding a condition for conditional formatting

> **Note**
>
> Not all visual types have the option for conditional formatting. The conditional formatting parameters will depend on the visual's type.

4. Next, click **Apply**. Once the setting has been applied, the visual will be reloaded and displayed, as shown in the following screenshot. Notice that the color changed to red since the value is less than the 95% threshold:

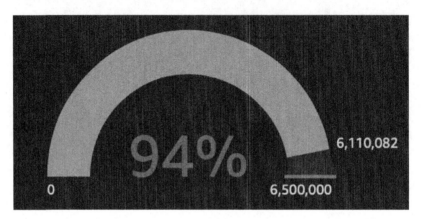

Figure 4.26 – Visual after conditional formatting has been applied

Feel free to try out different visual types and different conditions and settings.

Summary

Congratulations on completing this chapter. In this chapter, we learned how to create analyses, which is the main user interface for BI developers. We added the most common visual types that answer the most common questions in BI applications, such as visualizing **KPIs**, categories, and time series data. After we completed an analysis, we learned how to export an analysis into a dashboard and share it with business users.

Finally, we learned how to change the look and feel of our dashboards by applying themes or changing the colors of each visual independently and applying conditional formatting. With the knowledge obtained in this chapter, you can build meaningful visualizations for your business using QuickSight.

In the next chapter, we will learn how to build richer BI applications by adding interactivity to our dashboards.

Q&A

1. What is a visual in Amazon QuickSight?

2. What visual types are better fits for visualizing time series data?

3. Can you give some examples where conditional formatting is particularly useful?

4. How can you create and apply a custom theme?

5. What is a Sankey diagram and when would you use it?

Further reading

For more information regarding what was covered in this chapter, take a look at the following resource:

- *QuickSight User Guide* – AWS: `https://docs.aws.amazon.com/quicksight/latest/user/amazon-quicksight-user.pdf`

Section 2: Advanced Dashboarding and Insights

In this section, we will dive deeper into some more advanced features of Amazon QuickSight that will allow the reader to develop interactive and embedded dashboards and add machine learning capabilities to their dashboards.

This section consists of the following chapters:

- *Chapter 5, Building Interactive Dashboards*
- *Chapter 6, Working with ML Capabilities and Insights*
- *Chapter 7, Understanding Embedded Analytics*

5
Building Interactive Dashboards

In this chapter, we will learn how to develop interactive dashboards with Amazon QuickSight. You will learn how to add custom controls to your dashboards and add interactivity to your BI application using parameters. We will also look at advanced filtering options with point and click actions, as well as URL actions.

In this chapter, we will cover the following topics:

- Using filters and parameters
- Working with QuickSight Actions

Technical requirements

For this chapter, you will need the following:

- An AWS account
- A QuickSight account with the Author and Reader users configured
- The dashboard we created in *Chapter 4, Developing Visuals and Dashboards*

Using filters and parameters

Users can interact with dashboards by clicking on specific areas of the application or hovering over a visual to get additional information on specific data points. As a BI developer, you might come across scenarios where you will need to add additional interactivity to your dashboards, allowing your users to filter datasets or implement specific actions. In this section, we will learn how to leverage those specific QuickSight features to add interactivity to our dashboards. We will provide hands-on examples while using the New York dataset and dashboard we developed earlier in *Chapter 4, Developing Visuals and Dashboards*. But first, we will need to understand how to use QuickSight filters.

Working with filters

QuickSight authors can filter datasets. For example, you can use filtering when you need to refine a dataset before you visualize it. You can control the scope of the QuickSight filters so that they can be applied to the visuals you want. Filtering, when applied to a QuickSight analysis, is transparent from the reader's perspective. You can apply additional settings when sharing a dashboard with your readers if you need to allow your readers to filter data. Let's look at an example to understand how to add and apply filters. For our example, let's assume that we have detected `null` values and that we want to remove them from certain visuals:

1. First, we will need to open our New York Taxi analysis.

2. We will use the pivot table we created earlier. When we open the Borough category, we can observe the `null` value as the payment type. null values can be useful as they can help us detect issues with our data. For this example, let's assume we don't want to visualize the `null` values in the pivot table while keeping the rest of the visuals unaffected:

Fare amounts by borough and payment type		
Pick Up Borough	**Payment Type**	**Fare Amount**
⊟ **Bronx**	*null*	$969,806.58
	Cash	$50,961.67
	Credit Card	$100,715.51
	Dispute	-$334.70
	No Charge	$1,036.51
	Subtotal	$1,122,185.57
⊞ **Brooklyn**		$2,172,314.53

Figure 5.1 – Pivot table with null values

3. Select the pivot table by clicking on the visual. Then, select the filter tab from the left-hand side menu, as shown in the following screenshot:

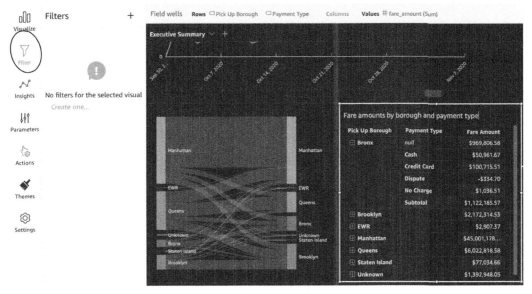

Figure 5.2 – Select visual for filtering

4. Since we have no filtering, we will get a prompt to create one. Click on the **Create one…** prompt and then select the filter you need to filter against (**Payment Type**, in this example).

5. This action will create a filter. Click on the newly created filter to get the filter configuration options.

6. Now that we created the filter, we need to confirm its scope. By default, a filter is only applied to the selected visual. The filter will not be applied to the entire analysis. We can change the scope of a filter if we need to add more visuals to its scope.

7. Next, we will need to define the conditions of the filtering. For our example, we will add a condition that *excludes* the NULL values, as shown here:

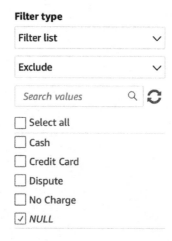

Figure 5.3 – Defining filter conditions

8. Click **Apply** and observe how the NULL values are excluded from our visual. Note that the rest of the visuals that are outside of the scope of our filter remain unchanged.

By default, filters don't appear on the reader user interface. Some BI applications might need to give users the ability to filter data.

> **Note**
>
> When filtering a dataset, QuickSight will query the dataset and then apply filtering. If your dataset has been configured as a direct query, QuickSight will connect to the data source to fetch the latest data before filtering. If your dataset is configured as a SPICE dataset, then QuickSight will fetch the data directly from SPICE, without the need to query or import data from the original data source.

To allow our reader users to filter data, we need to check the **Enable ad hoc filtering** option on the dashboard publishing screen. This option can be found under **Advanced publish options**, as shown here:

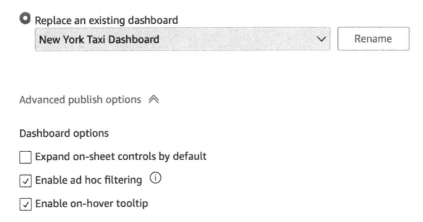

Figure 5.4 – Enable ad hoc filtering

Now that we have learned how to add a filter, let's introduce the concept of QuickSight parameters.

Working with parameters

Parameters in QuickSight are variables that a user can set, commonly using on-screen controls. A parameter can be used in various ways. For example, we can filter the analysis data dynamically based on a parameter. To understand this concept, we will use our example New York taxi analysis. Let's assume that our business users need to understand patterns and changes in customer behaviors based on what payment type the customers are using. To implement this use case, we will create a parameter that will store the user selection for the Payment Type field.

Creating a parameter

Creating a parameter is straightforward, as shown here:

1. You can either select the **Parameter** item on the left-hand side menu or click the **+ Add** button at the top right-hand side of the screen and then select **Add parameter**. Once selected, you will see the parameter creation screen, as shown here:

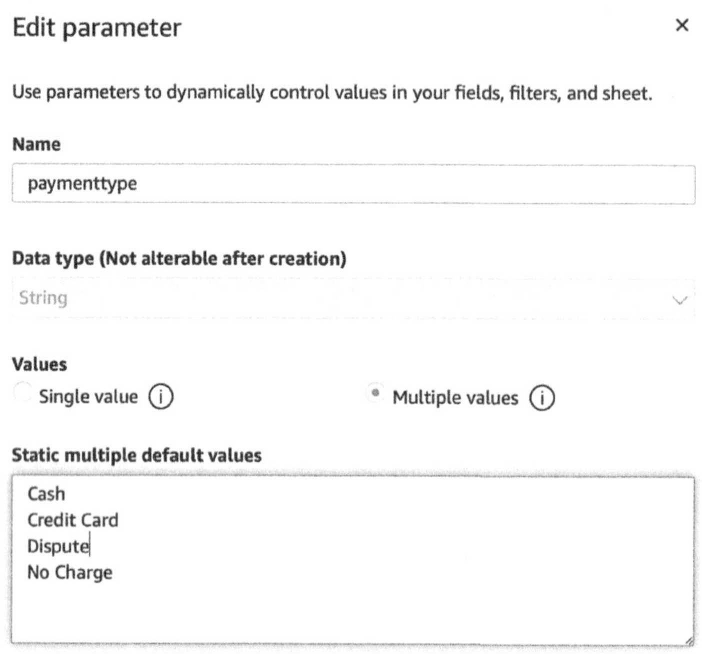

Figure 5.5 – Adding parameters

2. For this example, we will use the following values (as shown in the preceding screenshot):

    - **Name** : `paymenttype`
    - **Data type**: String
    - **Values**: Multiple values
    - **Default values**: `Cash`, `Credit Card`, `Dispute`, `No Charge`

3. Next, click **Create**. The parameter should now be added to your analysis.

At this stage, our parameter has been added to the analysis, but we are not using it yet. Next, we will link this parameter to the filter we created earlier.

Linking parameters to filters

While we are still on the analysis and logged in as the author user, to link parameters to filters, we will need to do the following:

1. First, locate the filter we created earlier. You can click on the visual where the filter has been applied and then click on the filters item on the left-hand side menu.

2. Now click **Edit**, or simply click on the **Payment Type** filter we created earlier.

3. To link a filter with a parameter, we will need to select **Custom filter** from the **Filter Type** drop-down menu.

4. Next, tick the **Use parameters** checkbox.

5. Next, there will be a pop-up, asking if you want to change the scope of your filter. Since we don't need to filter other visuals from our analysis, we will select **No**.

> **Note**
>
> The scope of the filter can be edited at any time once the parameter has been created. The scope update will have an immediate effect, without the need to update the parameters or your controls.

6. From the drop-down menu, select the `paymenttype` parameter we created earlier. The following screenshot shows what the filter configuration will look like when linking a filter to a parameter:

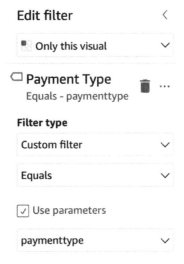

Figure 5.6 – Linking filters to parameters

7. Click **Apply** and then **Close**.

Now that our filter and parameter are connected, the filter will inherit the default values of our parameter. In our example, we have used a multi-value parameter. We can confirm that the pivot table only displays the records that contain the default values of the parameter. Now that we have linked the parameter with the visual, we will learn how to add on-screen controls and allow readers to change the parameter value.

Adding on-screen controls

QuickSight allows you to add on-screen controls so that your reader users can set the value of a parameter dynamically. In our example, setting the `paymenttype` parameter value will result in changes in the value of the **Payment Type** filter, which has been applied to the pivot table visual. To add an onscreen control, follow these steps:

1. First, select the **Parameters** item from the left-hand side menu.

2. Then, select the **paymenttype** parameter we created earlier. From the drop-down menu, click **Add control**, as shown here:

Figure 5.7 – Adding on-screen controls

3. From the control's creation settings, we will need to define the following parameters:

    • **Display Name**: A user-friendly name for the on-screen control. In our example, we used `Payment Type`.

    • **Style**: The type of control that your users will be using to set the parameter. The control styles options are also determined by the data type of the parameter. For example, if our parameter was a date type, **Date Picker** would be among the available options. For our example, we will use the **List – Multiselect** style, as shown in the following screenshot. This type will allow our users to select multiple values from a drop-down menu.

- **Values**: The values that the users can select from. You can link these values to values from a dataset, which ensures that the available values are synced with the dataset, so there isn't a need to maintain these values separately. In our example, we linked the values of the `Payment Type` field. The following screenshot shows an example of an on-screen control configuration:

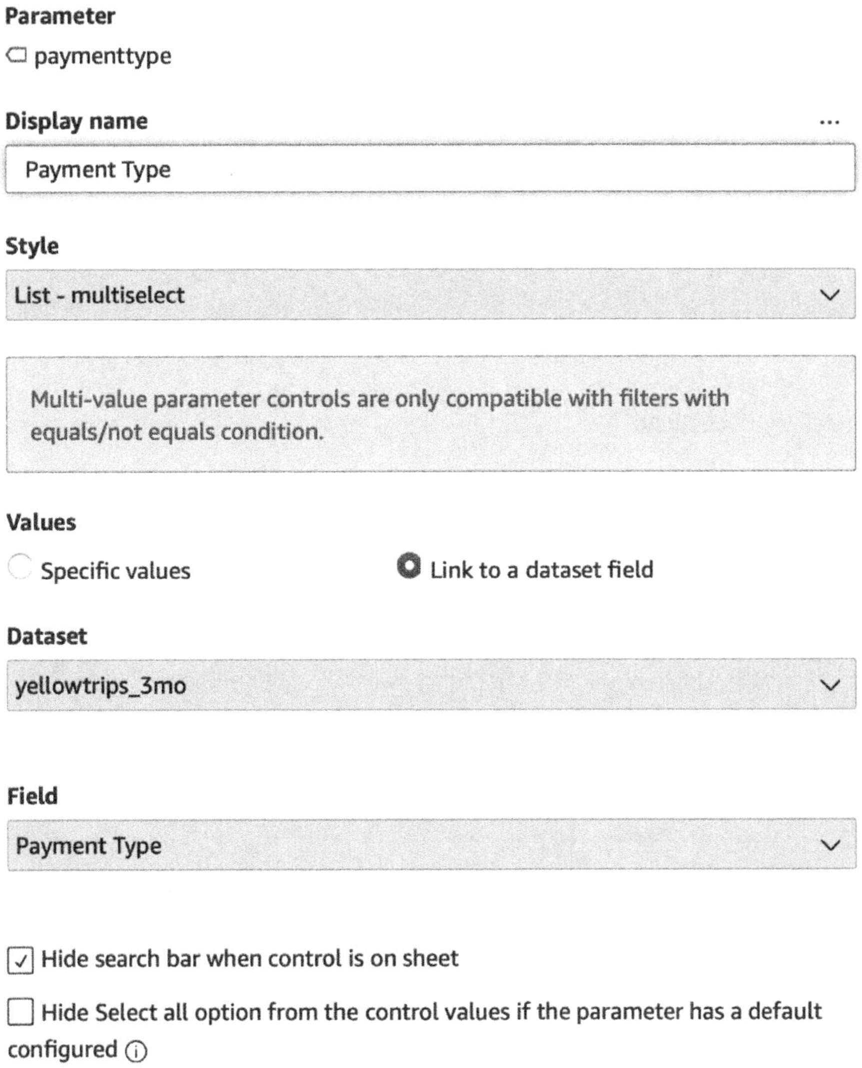

Parameter

▭ paymenttype

Display name   ...

Payment Type

Style

List - multiselect	∨

Multi-value parameter controls are only compatible with filters with equals/not equals condition.

Values

○ Specific values   ◉ Link to a dataset field

Dataset

yellowtrips_3mo	∨

Field

Payment Type	∨

☑ Hide search bar when control is on sheet

☐ Hide Select all option from the control values if the parameter has a default configured ⓘ

Figure 5.8 – Adding on-screen controls to the parameter

4. Click **Apply** to add the on-screen control.

Now that we've added the on-screen control, we have all the required components that allow us to publish interactive dashboards. Let's look at the sequence of events that enable interactivity on our dashboards:

1. First, the user selects values using on-screen controls.

2. The selected values are passed to parameters.

3. Then, these parameters are used as filter conditions.

4. Finally, the visuals in the scope of the filter are updated after user selections.

    The following diagram depicts the flow described here:

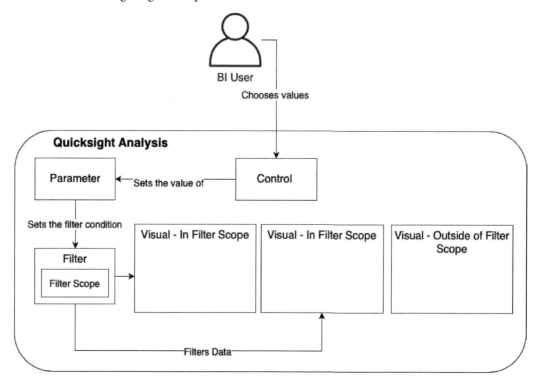

Figure 5.9 – Components for interactive filtering

Now that we have configured all the required components, let's test the on-screen controls:

1. First, notice that at the top of the screen, we have a new section named **Controls**, under which we have the newly created **Payment Type** on-screen control. The following screenshot shows the newly created control:

Figure 5.10 – Multi-select control

2. Changing the selection of this control will automatically change the values of the `paymenttype` parameter, which was configured to work with our Payment Type filter.

3. You can access additional options from the on-filter controls. One of the options that's available allows you to detach the control from the top of the screen and add it to the analysis sheet. This is a good option for filters that have a narrow scope. In our example, our filter covers only a single visual, so placing the control next to the visual might provide a better overall user experience while saving screen estate at the top of the screen. The following screenshot shows the on-screen control being placed next to the pivot table:

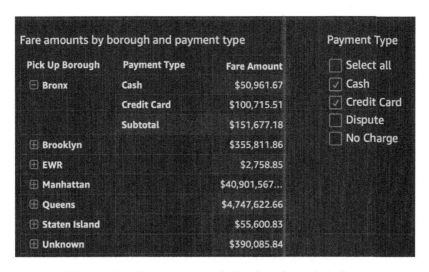

Figure 5.11 – On-screen control placed on the analysis sheet

Now that we have configured the analysis and arranged the onscreen controls, we can publish the analysis as a dashboard and share it with our reader users. With that, we have created our first truly interactive QuickSight dashboard. Next, we will learn how to use actions to add more interactive controls to our dashboards.

Working with actions

QuickSight Actions allow you to add interactivity to your dashboards. They can be any of the following:

- **Filter actions**
- **Navigation actions**
- **URL actions**

Next, we will look closer at each of these action types. To understand each type, we will configure them using our New York taxi sample analysis.

Working with filter actions

URL actions allow us to instantly filter data when the user clicks on a specific area of a dashboard. Filter actions make it easier for your readers to focus on specific data points of the analysis.

When configuring filter actions, you will need to choose a visual in your analysis and then provide the following information:

- **Action Name**: A user-friendly and descriptive name for the filter action.
- **Activation**: **Menu Option** or **Select**: **Menu Option** will add a menu item when you click a data point in your visual. This option, when clicked, will activate the URL action. On the other hand, with the **Select** option, your URL action will be activated directly when you click a data point.
- **Filter scope**: Which visuals will be filtered.

To understand filter actions, we will use an example from our New York Taxi analysis. Let's assume that we want our users to instantly focus on a specific borough and update the KPI and Sankey visual to reflect the selected borough only. To select a borough, we will use the bar chart diagram that displays the average tip per borough, which we configured in *Chapter 4, Developing Visuals and Dashboards*:

1. First, navigate to the analysis and select the bar chart visual by simply clicking on it.
2. Next, with the visual selected, click on **Actions** from the left-hand side menu.

3. Click **Add action** and then **Filter action** from the **Action Type** drop-down menu.

4. Add the values shown in the following screenshot:

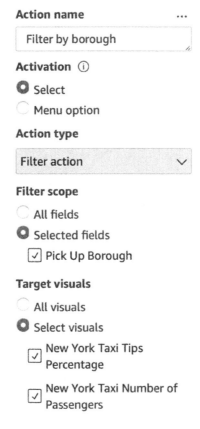

Figure 5.12 – Filter action

We'll update the following parameters:

- **Action name**: `Filter by borough`

- **Activation**: **Select**

- **Filter scope**: Selected fields

- **Target visuals**: The KPI and Sankey visuals

5.   Click **Save**.

The filter action has now been applied. To quickly test the newly created action, just click on any Pickup Borough data point on the bar chart and notice how the target visuals update. For example, with the Queens borough selected, we can see an example of how the Sankey diagram looks, as follows:

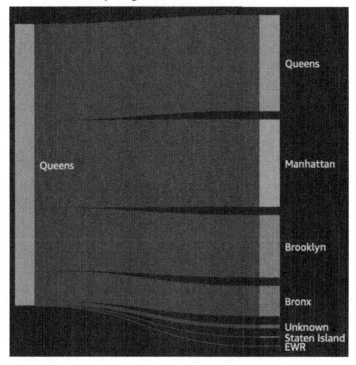

Figure 5.13 – Sankey diagram once the filter action has been applied

Feel free to try adding add more filter actions to other visuals in your analysis. Next, we will learn how to configure navigation actions.

Working with navigation actions

As you are adding visuals to analysis, it can reach a point when there might be too many visuals for a single page. In these scenarios, you can organize visuals into sheets. For each sheet, you can provide a user-friendly name to help your BI users navigate the dashboard. For each sheet, you can provide the following details:

- **Title**
- **Description**

Both can help give your users context. Title and description can be particularly useful in scenarios where there are many sheets. Navigation actions can help you define actions that will allow your users to quickly navigate to different sheets within the same analysis.

When configuring navigation actions, you will need to choose a visual in your analysis and then provide the following information:

- **Action name**: The name of the navigation action.

- **Activation**: **Menu option** or **Select**: **Menu Option** will add a menu item when you click a data point in your visual. This option, when clicked, will activate the URL action. On the other hand, with the **Select** option, your URL action will be activated directly when you click a data point.

- **Target sheet**: The sheet name where your user redirects to when the action activates.

- **Parameters**: This lets the user set parameter values after navigating to the target sheet.

Next, we will look at another type of action: URL actions.

Working with URL actions

URL actions allow us to redirect our user to another website or another dashboard when the user clicks on a specific area of a dashboard. URL actions can help your BI users easily retrieve additional context for the dashboard.

When configuring URL actions, you will need to choose a visual in your analysis and then provide the following information:

- **Action Name**: A user-friendly and descriptive name for the URL action.

- **Activation**: **Menu Option** or **Select**: **Menu Option** will add a menu item when you click a data point in your visual. This option, when clicked, will activate the URL action. On the other hand, with the **Select** option, your URL action will be activated directly when you click a data point.

- **URL**: The URL where you want to redirect your user.

> **Note**
>
> You can add references to the parameters of field values in the URL field. This will allow you to redirect your users to different URLs, based on the user selection. The syntax to refer to a parameter is `<<$parameter-name>>`, while the syntax to refer to a field is `{{field-name}}`.

- **Open in**: This option determines how your browser will open the link from the URL actions. The options are opening in the *same tab*, opening in a *different tab*, or opening in a *different browser window*.

To understand how to set up URL actions, we will use our New York Taxi analysis. Let's assume that we need to add a link to an external website with additional information on each of the New York boroughs. For this example, we will use the bar chart visual we configured in *Chapter 4, Developing Visuals and Dashboards*. We will use Wikipedia as our external website:

1. First, navigate to the analysis and select the bar chart visual.

2. Next, with the visual selected, click on **Actions** from the left-hand side menu.

3. Click **Add** action and then select **URL action** from the **Action Type** drop-down menu.

4. Add the values shown in the following screenshot:

Figure 5.14 – URL action

These values are as follows:

- **Action name**: `Wikipedia look up`

- **Activation**: **Menu option**

- **URL**: `https://en.wikipedia.org/wiki/<<{Pick Up Borough}>>`

- **Open in**: New browser tab

5. Click **Save**.

The URL action has now been applied to our visual. To test URL actions, you need to click on the data points of the visual where you applied the action. In our example, every data point will redirect to a different URL, since we are using the `Pickup Borough` field as part of our URL. When you test something like this in the real world, you will need to ensure that each URL is redirecting the user correctly. The following screenshot is what we'll see upon right-clicking on the **Manhattan** bar in our bar chart. Notice that a **Wikipedia look up** menu option appears, which will redirect us to the Manhattan Wikipedia page (`https://en.wikipedia.org/wiki/Manhattan`) when we click on it:

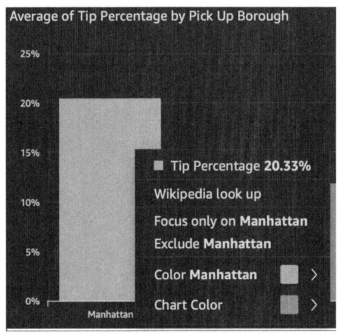

Figure 5.15 – URL action menu item

Thus, we have figured out how to work with various types of actions as well.

Summary

Congratulations on completing this chapter! In this chapter, we learned how to add interactivity to our dashboards. We learned how to add QuickSight parameters and on-screen controls to filter the data of our analysis following user input. We also learned how to configure the three types of actions: the filter action, the navigation action, and the URL action. Using these features, you will be able to create BI applications, with interactive controls enhancing the user experience of your BI applications. With the actions we learned about in this chapter, your users will be able to perform single-click filtering, navigate easily between multiple sheets, and open external websites that provide additional context.

In the next chapter, we will learn how to use insights and add machine learning to our analyses.

Q&A

1. What filter type can be linked to a parameter?

2. How can you use a parameter with a URL action?

3. When do we need to use sheets?

4. How can we help business users navigate between different sheets?

5. What is the difference between filter actions and navigation actions?

6. What is the difference between **Menu option** and **Select** for action activation?

Further reading

- *QuickSight User Guide* – AWS: https://docs.aws.amazon.com/ quicksight/latest/user/amazon-quicksight-user.pdf

6
Working with ML Capabilities and Insights

In this chapter, we will explore visual types in **Amazon QuickSight**. Using hands-on examples, we will add **machine learning** (**ML**) capabilities to our dashboards. More specifically, we will add forecasting for time series data and anomaly detection capabilities. To describe insights from the data, we will add natural language narratives in our dashboards.

In this chapter, we will cover the following topics:

- Using forecasting
- Working with insights
- Working with ML insights

Technical requirements

For this chapter, you will need the following:

- An **AWS** account
- A QuickSight account with **Author** and **Reader** users configured
- The datasets created in *Chapter 2, Introduction to Amazon QuickSight*
- The analysis created in *Chapter 3, Preparing Data with Amazon QuickSight*

Using forecasting

Amazon QuickSight allows you to add **forecasting** to your dashboards without the need to develop complex ML models. To better understand how to configure forecasting, we will use the example dataset we configured in *Chapter 2, Introduction to Amazon QuickSight*.

Adding forecasting

For our example, let's assume that we need to develop a dashboard that contains forecasts about the total number of taxi fares in the future. As expected, our data has a certain degree of seasonality. Also, we can see from the line chart visual we developed in *Chapter 3, Preparing Data with Amazon QuickSight*, that during Sundays, there is a drop in the total taxi fares compared to the other days of the week. Identifying the most appropriate seasonality for our dataset is not always straightforward. In our example, we have different levels of seasonality depending on what time interval we will consider. A season can be 24 hours, or a week, or a year. Identifying the right seasonality is important when configuring forecasts, as they can be used to more accurately predict future events and metrics.

Now, let's add forecasting in our *New York Taxi* analysis:

1. First, select the line chart diagram we developed in *Chapter 3, Preparing Data with Amazon QuickSight*.

> **Note**
> Not all visual types support forecasting. Line charts with a time dimension are very good candidates for forecasting, as they commonly visualize time series data.

2. Next, click on the visual settings and then click **Add forecast**, as shown here:

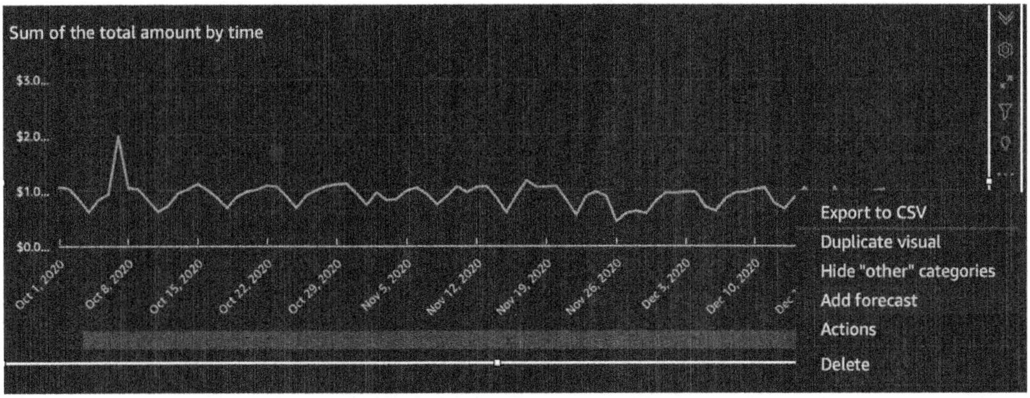

Figure 6.1 – Adding forecasts

3. Next, we will edit the forecasting parameters as follows:

- **Forecast length**: Periods forward/backward are the number of time intervals that you want to get a forecast for.

> **Note**
>
> When configuring forecasting periods, a period is matching the period of the visual where the forecasting is applied. For example, if your data is aggregated daily, then a period of seven (7) intervals equals 1 week. If your data is aggregated monthly, then a period will correspond to a month, therefore a period of 12 intervals will be a full year.

- **Prediction interval**: This represents the probability that the future values will be within the forecasted values.

> **Note**
>
> The prediction interval can be between 5% and 95%. The lower the prediction interval, the narrower the forecasting range will be.

- **Seasonality**: This is the time interval when your time series has predictable changes. By default, QuickSight will automatically identify the best seasonality pattern for your data. You can choose to override the automatic selection with a manual selection.

For our example, we will use the following values:

- **Periods forwards**: 30 – This will give us predictions for 1 month if our data is aggregated daily.

- **Periods backwards**: 0 – In this example, we are not interested in backward predictions.

- **Prediction interval**: 75 – We can start with 75 as a starting point, and then adjust.

- **Seasonality**: Automatic.

4. The forecasted area is shown as a range of values, highlighted with different colors. We can see the visual with forecasting as shown in the following figure:

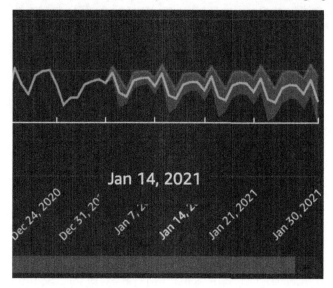

Figure 6.2 – Time series data with forecasting

Now that we have added forecasting capabilities to a line chart visual, in the next section, we will learn how to add different scenarios that can alter our forecasts, called what-if scenarios.

Working with what-if scenarios

What-if scenarios allow us to project a specific target in the future and then observe how this affects a forecast. To better understand the what-if analysis, we will use the forecast visual we just configured. Let's assume, because of a new initiative, taxi ridership is expected to increase, and by 15 January 2020, we will have at least a 2.5x increase. We can use this scenario to understand how this goal will affect our projections for the future:

1. First, to open the what-if analysis, we simply need to click on a data point in the forecast area.

2. Next, we will need to define our scenario. In our case, with 15 Jan, 2021 selected, we simply add our target value as $2,500,000, which is more than double the original forecast.

3. Click **Apply** and then observe that we have a second forecast line that corresponds to the scenario of having increased revenue. The original forecast can be observed too with the dotted lines. See the following figure for an example of a what-if scenario:

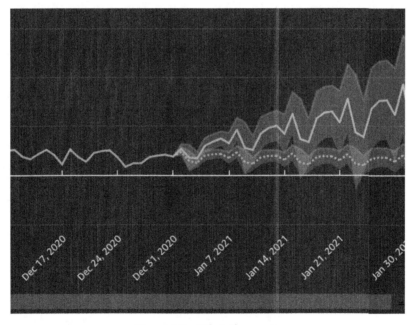

Figure 6.3 – What-if scenario

Congratulations, you have added a what-if analysis with only a few clicks. Next, we will learn how to use insights, which are a special type of QuickSight visual that allow you to describe your insights from your data using natural language.

Working with insights

QuickSight **insights** offer a set of features that allow you to express insights from data using natural language. QuickSight can automatically interpret a diagram and suggest narratives that you can quickly add to your analysis. In addition to that, you can build your own custom narrative. In this section, we will do the following:

- Learn how to use suggested insights.

- Create and edit a custom insight.

Adding suggested insights

To better understand the **autonarrative** features, we will use the example *New York Taxi* analysis. Let's start with the Sankey diagram to discover interesting insights from the data:

1. First, open the analysis and select any visual by clicking on it.

2. Next, click on the insights icon to reveal the **Suggested insights** list, as shown here:

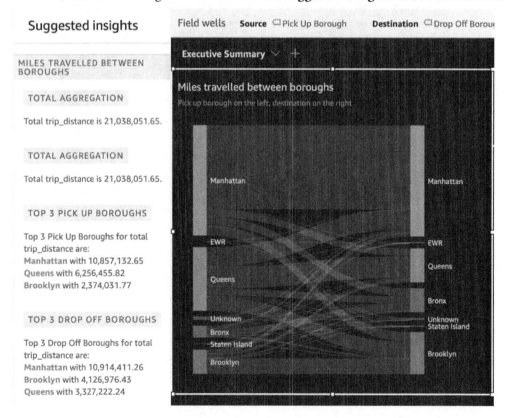

Figure 6.4 – Selecting the suggested insights

Next, we will select an insight that looks interesting to display. For example, we can display the days with the highest and lowest taxi fares over the entire period we are visualizing.

3. Scroll down to find the **WORST DAY** insight and then click the plus icon to add the insight to your analysis.

4. Repeat *Step 3* for the **BEST DAY** insight.

5. Resize and format the insights.

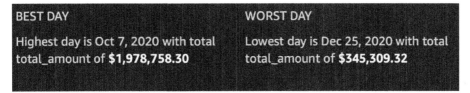

BEST DAY

Highest day is Oct 7, 2020 with total total_amount of **$1,978,758.30**

WORST DAY

Lowest day is Dec 25, 2020 with total total_amount of **$345,309.32**

Figure 6.5 – Adding suggested insights

Interestingly, Christmas day happens to be the day with the least taxi fares. Feel free to explore and familiarize yourself with the other narrative suggestions. In the next section, we will learn how to create a new narrative manually, which is particularly useful when you need a different narrative from those autosuggested, and need to control the text displayed by customizing your narrative.

Creating and editing an insight

In this section, we will learn how to create and edit a custom insight. To better understand how to set it up, we will use the New York dataset analysis. Let's assume that we want to display the total number of miles traveled by New York taxis and display it on the screen using natural language. For example, consider the following:

```
The total distance traveled in New York over the period between
<Start Date> to <End Date> was <number> miles.
```

In the next section, we will learn how to develop an insight that answers the previous questions.

Adding an insight

In this section, we will start by learning how to add an insight in Amazon QuickSight:

1. First, click on the **+ Add** button and then select **Add Insight**.

2. Next, we will need to select the computation type for our insight, as shown in the following figure:

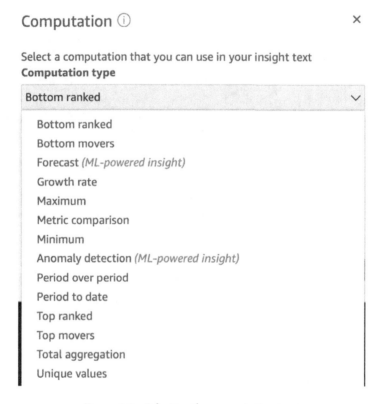

Figure 6.6 – Selecting the computation type

3. Select the **Total aggregation** computation type, since our problem is a total aggregation of the `trip_distance` field, which represents the total miles traveled.

4. Now, we need to choose the fields from our dataset to populate our insight. Selecting fields is similar to how we were selecting fields for our visuals, by dragging and dropping the values into the **Field Well** area of the screen at the top of the analysis. For our calculation, we need to select `trip_distance` (Sum) as the **Values** field and leave the **Time** and **Categories** fields empty.

5. Now, the insight should appear as follows:

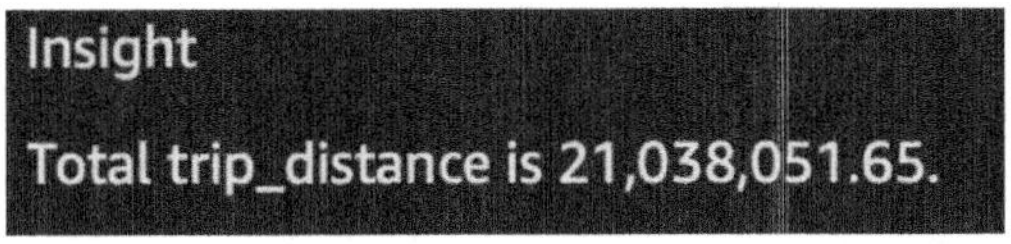

Insight

Total trip_distance is 21,038,051.65.

Figure 6.7 – Total aggregation insight

Now, we have managed to add the insight into our analysis. We now need to edit it so that it matches the narrative we were aiming for. In the next section, we will learn how to edit an insight.

Editing an insight

When adding elements to your narrative, you can automatically add the following:

- **Computations**: Predefined calculations
- **Parameters**: Variables that you can set in your analysis
- **Functions**: Used to change a field into the desired format

To better understand how to use these terms, we will edit our example narrative:

1. First, let's add two new parameters, DateStart and DateEnd, as we learned in *Chapter 5, Building Interactive Dashboards*. Set the default value to 01 October 2020 for the DateStart parameter and 31 December 2020 for the DateEnd parameter.

2. Connect these parameters to a filter, and use the **Pick Date** field to control the parameter value. Make sure that the filter scope includes the insight visual.

3. Now that we have the two parameters set up, we will edit the narrative.

To edit an insight, we need to click on the insight settings by hovering over the right-hand side of the insight, clicking on the ... icon, and then selecting **Customize narrative** to open the **narrative expression editor**, shown as follows:

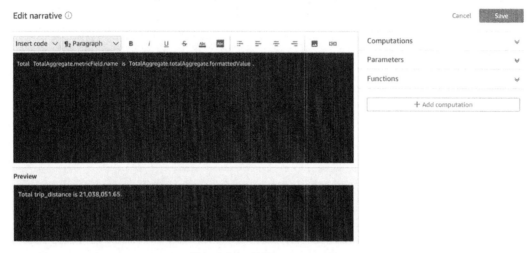

Figure 6.8 – Editing a narrative

Note, the narrative contains `Total TotalAggregate.metricField.name is TotalAggregate.totalAggregate.formattedValue`. We can alter this text so that we can achieve the desired narrative.

For our target narrative, we will need to see something like the following:

```
"The total distance traveled in New York over the period
between 01 Oct 2020 and 31 Dec 2020 is 21,036,854.06 miles."
```

From the previous step, we already have the total number of miles as `TotalAggregate.totalAggregate.formattedValue`. To reach our target narrative, we will need to do the following:

1. Customize the remaining text.
2. Add the two date parameters.
3. Convert the date into the desired date format.

Starting with the text, we need to replace the existing text with the following:

```
"The total distance traveled in New York over the period
between <> and <> is TotalAggregate.totalAggregate.
formattedValue miles."
```

Next, we will add the two date parameters. You can access the **Parameters** menu on the right-hand side of the screen and simply add the two parameters.

Note, the expression will look like `${DateStart}`. Observe **Preview**, which is located below the editor. You might notice that the time is displayed in the epoch format, which is not what the end user would expect. For that reason, we will need to covert the date into a format that is understandable by the end user. To change the format, we will use the `formatDate` function. You can locate the function by expanding the **Functions** menu on the right-hand side menu and selecting `formatDate`. The function expects two arguments:

- The date column
- The format expressed as a string

In our example, we will use the `dd MMM yyyy` format, and therefore, the function will be `formatDate(${DateStart},'dd MMM yyyy')` for the start date and `formatDate(${DateEnd},'dd MMM yyyy')` for the end date.

Now that we have added the start and end date, the text will be as follows:

The total distance traveled in New York over the period between `formatDate(${DateStart},'dd MMM yyyy')` and `formatDate(${DateEnd},'dd MMM yyyy')` is `TotalAggregate.totalAggregate.formattedValue` miles.

Finally, use the editor to edit the text format. For example, we can change the color of the number of miles and make the start and end date text bold for emphasis. After applying these changes, click **Save**. The narrative will look like the following:

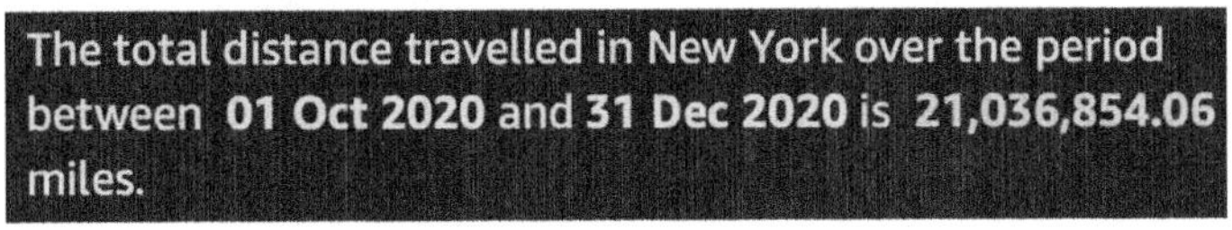

The total distance travelled in New York over the period between **01 Oct 2020** and **31 Dec 2020** is **21,036,854.06** miles.

Figure 6.9 – Insight with a customized narrative

Narratives can be really useful to describe important insights from the data using natural language. With the QuickSight editor, we have full control over how the text is displayed to the end user. Now that we have learned how to work with and customize insights, in the next section, we will learn how to use ML-driven insights.

Working with ML insights

QuickSight has a special type of insight where the results are driven from ML-based computations. QuickSight supports two types of ML insights:

- Forecasting
- Anomaly detection

In the next section, we will learn how to configure each of these types of insights.

Working with forecasting insights

We learned how to add forecasting in a line graph visual. QuickSight also allows you to add forecasting as a narrative to display forecasted values. For example, how many miles is expected to be traveled between Manhattan and Queens on a specific date?

To better understand how to configure this type of visual, we will use our example *New York Taxi* analysis to answer this question:

1. First, let's create a new insight and select **Forecast ML-Powered Insight** from the drop-down list.

2. For this example, let's assume that we want the user to choose the pick-up borough and the destination borough (drop-off borough). To achieve this, we will create two filter parameters (let's name them `PickUpBoroughForecast` and `DropOffBoroughForecast`) with on-screen controls that allow the user to select the pick-up and drop-off boroughs, as we learned in *Chapter 4, Developing Visuals and Dashboards*. Make sure the filter applies only to the newly created forecast insight so that it is not affecting the other visuals in our analysis.

3. Now, let's focus on the ML forecast visual. Let's assume that we need to estimate the total miles driven between Manhattan and Queens on the 10 January, which is 10 days after our latest data point.

4. Select the `Pick Up Time` value as the **Time** field and the `trip_distance (sum)` value as the **Value** field. Now, the forecasting visual should automatically display text like the following:

    ```
    Total trip_distance is forecasted to be
    4,546.560032279868 for Jan 14, 2021
    ```

5. Now, we will need to customize the narrative to ensure it displays the text we need and the forecast time is what we expect.

6. In the narrative editor, we will alter the text and include the two parameters. We can optionally round the miles to the nearest integer. After these changes, the narrative should look like the following:

```
Total distance driven from ${PickUpBoroughForecast}
to ${DropOffBoroughForecast} on the ForecastInsight.
timeValue.formattedValue is forecasted to be
round(ForecastInsight.metricValue.value,0) miles.
```

7. Next, we need to ensure that the forecast parameters are correct. To access the forecast parameters, click the pencil icon next to the **ForecastInsight** computation, as shown here:

Figure 6.10 – Accessing the ForecastInsight parameters

8. In the next screen, ensure that the forecast length is set as 10 for the **forward period** and 0 for the **backward period**.

9. Optionally, edit the text styling. After these changes, the forecast insight, including the two onscreen controls, will look like the following:

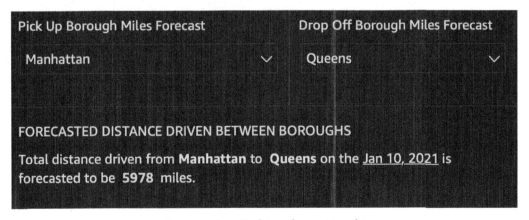

Figure 6.11 – ML-driven forecast insight

With this visual, our end users can choose any pick-up borough and drop-off borough and easily access ML forecasts generated by QuickSight, and get it displayed back to them in natural language. Now that we've learned how to add forecasting insights, in the next section, we will learn how to work with another type of ML-driven insight – the **anomaly detection insight**.

Working with anomaly detection insights

QuickSight also allows you to add anomaly detection insights and explore anomalies. For example, are there any dates where taxi traffic is lower than normal?

Adding and editing anomaly detection insights

To better understand how to configure this type of visual, we will use our *New York Taxi* analysis:

1. First, let's create a new insight and select **Anomaly Detection (ML-powered Insight)** from the drop-down menu.

2. Now, we need to choose the fields for our newly created insight. Set the **Time** field as `Pick Up Time` and the **Value** field as `trip_distance(sum)`.

3. Next, we need to configure our anomaly detection. Click on **Get started**, as shown here:

Figure 6.12 – Get started with anomaly detection

4. Next, on the anomaly detection configuration page, leave everything as is for now. Add `Pick Up Borough`, `Drop Off Borough`, `Pick Up Zone`, and `Drop Off Zone` as the four contributor fields. Before you click **Save**, let's observe the key components of this page, shown as follows:

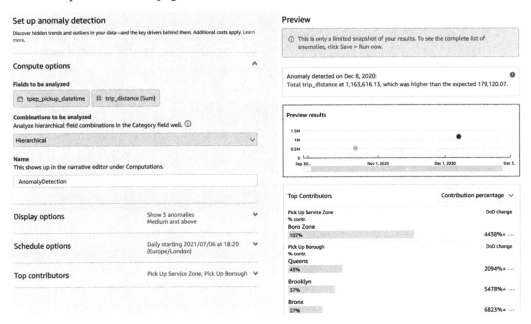

Figure 6.13 – Set up anomaly detection page

On the left-hand side, we have all the settings, and on the right-hand side, we have the **Preview** screen. The **Preview** screen can help us instantly understand the impact of any changes we are applying. Looking at the settings, you can select the hierarchy of analyzed fields (this doesn't apply in our example, since we only use a single **Time** field and a single **Value** field, without any dimension). You can also configure the display options, and determine what anomalies need to be displayed. You can schedule the ML job, and you can also define fields that are considered **contributors** to an outlier. These fields will later be used for **contribution analysis** when an anomaly is detected.

5. Next, click **Save**, and then run the ML analysis to generate the anomalies. After a couple of minutes, our insight will be populated with any anomalies found. See the following screenshot as an example:

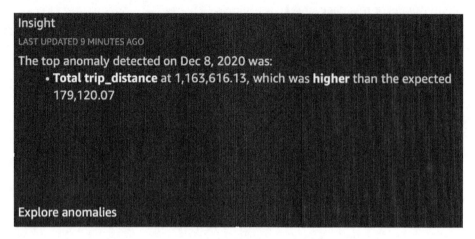

Figure 6.14 – Anomaly detection insight example

6. Similarly to other narratives, we can customize this narrative so that we can display the text we want to be displayed to our end users. For now, we will leave the autogenerated text. Let's observe the anomaly identified – on a particular date (8 December), there were over six times more miles driven than expected.

Note the **Explore anomalies** button at the bottom of the anomaly detection insight. In the next section, we will learn how to explore anomalies and perform contributor analysis.

Exploring anomalies

QuickSight offers users a tool to explore anomalies and understand contributing factors to outliers. To better understand this capability, we will use the anomaly detection insight we configured in the previous section. Click on **Explore anomalies** at the bottom of the ML-powered insight to access this user interface:

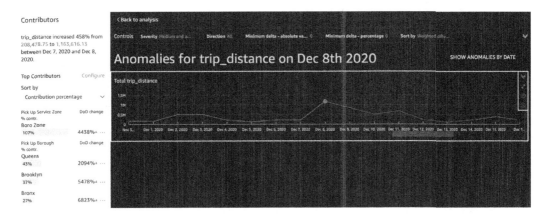

Figure 6.15 – Explore anomalies

On the top of the screen, we can choose our settings to determine what anomalies will be displayed. We can choose from the following:

- **Severity**: This determines how sensitive our algorithm is when detecting anomalies.

- **Direction**: This determines whether we are interested in higher-than-expected values, lower-than-expected values, or both.

- **Minimum delta** (absolute value or percentage): This allows us to set a specific value or percentage to determine a threshold for anomaly detection.

For this example, we don't need to change these values. We can focus on the left-hand side of the screen and see the contributors to the anomaly. We can rank their contribution to the anomaly and sort them by the following criteria:

- Deviation from expected

- Absolute difference

- Contribution percentage

- Percentage difference

Now, let's observe what kind of insight we get using the data from our example. When we sort by contribution percentage, we can observe that the Boro Zone for both the pick-up and drop-off zone is contributing significantly more to the total miles compared to normal. In regard to boroughs, Queens is coming in front as the largest difference in contribution as the pick-up borough and Manhattan Beach and Crown Heights North as the largest difference in contribution for drop-off borough. The results we get are consistent when we sort the contributors by **Deviation from expected**. I am not sure whether there was any significant event on that day in New York, but we can certainly easily see that there was some unusual taxi data on that Sunday.

Summary

Congratulations on completing this chapter. In this chapter, we learned how to add ML capabilities to our dashboards. We learned how to add forecasting, including building complex scenarios with what-if analysis. We also learned how to configure narratives and customize them using the QuickSight narrative editor. Finally, we learned how to create outlier detections and perform contributor analysis for anomaly detection. With the capabilities we learned in this chapter, your users will be able to get access to rich visuals and narratives in natural language with simple calculations or more sophisticated ML-driven calculations.

At this stage, we have learned about most of the capabilities of QuickSight analysis, and by combining the knowledge you have learned so far in this book you can configure complex dashboards that provide rich insights for your business users. In the next chapter, we will learn how to embed these dashboards into your own custom application.

Questions

1. What are the most appropriate visual types to add forecasting?
2. What are the QuickSight narratives and when should we use them?
3. When should we use ML insights versus simpler computations for our insights?
4. What are the contributors when configuring anomaly detection in QuickSight?
5. How can we access the outlier detection application?

Further reading

*   *Amazon QuickSight User Guide*:

    ```
    https://docs.aws.amazon.com/quicksight/latest/user/amazon-
    quicksight-user.pdf
    ```

7
Understanding Embedded Analytics

In this chapter, we will understand the embedded capabilities of Amazon QuickSight. We will discuss the business drivers for embedded analytics, and we will take a closer look at its architecture. Finally, throughout this chapter, we will provide hands-on examples to help you understand how to set up embedded analytics.

In this chapter, we will cover the following topics:

- Introducing QuickSight embedded analytics
- Architecture and user authentication
- Generating an embedded dashboard URL

Technical requirements

For this chapter, you will need the following:

- An AWS account with administrator permissions
- A QuickSight account with the Author and Reader users configured
- The dashboards we created in *Chapter 4*, *Developing Visuals and Dashboards*

Introducing QuickSight embedded analytics

So far in this book, we have learned how to create dashboards and work with analyses within the native QuickSight web application. For many use cases, this is sufficient. On the other hand, some organizations need to add data visualizations to an existing web portal, outside of the native QuickSight application.

Understanding the business drivers for embedding

Before embedding, organizations needed to develop their own custom **Business Intelligence (BI)** solutions. **D3.js** (https://d3js.org) is an open source JavaScript library for data visualizations on the web. D3.js requires a high level of expertise. This can be hard to find, making it challenging for many organizations to adopt this technology. While there are numerous examples on the web regarding how to build D3.js visualizations (https://observablehq.com/@d3/gallery), JavaScript can be a difficult language to learn for BI developers. At the same time, web developers might not have a deep understanding of the organization's data, which would enable them to choose the right visualizations for the questions they are trying to get answers for, as well as insights from the data. On top of this, when building embedded BI solutions, organizations need to consider other aspects, such as the following:

- How do we fetch data from the datastore?
- How frequently do we need to fetch new data?
- How many users are going to access the application?

QuickSight can directly address these challenges with dashboard embedding. Instead of developing custom visualization components, you can request data visualizations using the QuickSight API and embed them into your HTML code. QuickSight is a fully managed AWS service and will scale automatically for the number of users, enabling organizations and BI developers to focus their efforts on building dashboards rather than scaling their BI solution. For these reasons, embedded dashboards can be an efficient and simple-to-use solution when organizations need to leverage the scale of the AWS cloud for their BI solution, which is embedded into their web applications. Next, we will distinguish between the two types of embedded analytics supported by QuickSight.

Understanding embedded analytics types

There are two different embedded capabilities Amazon QuickSight supports:

- **Read-only dashboard embedding**
- **QuickSight console embedding**

Understanding read-only dashboard embedding

You can embed read-only dashboards into your web applications. This type of embedding can be used to add **read-only** visuals to your custom portal application and expose it to internal or external users. Users that access embedded dashboards have a similar experience to the one when accessing a QuickSight dashboard via the web application, as shown in *Chapter 3*, *Preparing Data with Amazon QuickSight*. While users can view the visuals, as well as drill down or select specific datapoints or categories, they don't have access to the authoring interface and dataset creation processes. In this mode, visual creation, dataset setup, and all the other operations that an author user can complete can only be completed using the QuickSight web app. For read-only dashboard embedding, your users can be authenticated, or you can enable **anonymous** access to allow unauthenticated users to view the dashboards. The latter is a good option when you don't need your users to be authenticated to access dashboards, such as when you need to embed your dashboard into a public-facing website.

> **Note**
> To enable anonymous access, your QuickSight admin needs to enable **session capacity planning**. With session capacity planning, you can buy several sessions, based on the traffic expected for your dashboard. Each session is a 30-minute usage block.

The embedded dashboard is in the form of a URL with an authorization code. To get the embedded dashboard URL, you will need to call the `GetDashboardEmbedUrl` API call. This API call returns a session URL with an authorization code that can be used to embed the dashboard into your website. The `GetDashboardEmbedUrl` API call needs to be initiated by the web application server, not from the user's browser. To add an embedded dashboard URL to your website, you can use the `embedDashboard(options)` method from the **QuickSight Embedding SDK**. This allows you to easily set a parameter value so that your dashboard starts with specific initial parameters. Other options include the embedded frame formatting, allow/not allow printing, scrolling behavior, and starting sheet. For more information, you can read the QuickSight Embedding SDK documentation: `https://github.com/awslabs/amazon-QuickSight-embedding-sdk`.

Understanding QuickSight console embedding

You can embed the full QuickSight console application into your web application. The embedded console capabilities are only available to authenticated QuickSight users. As expected, anonymous access is not an option for this type of embedding. Similar to the QuickSight web app, only authenticated users can access the QuickSight console. Console embedding will provide your users with the full QuickSight experience. You will be able to have both reader and author users using it. Authors will be able to configure datasets, perform analysis, and share dashboards, while your readers will be able to access read-only dashboards. The console session is in the form of a URL with an authorization code. To get the console embedding URL, you will need to use the QuickSight `GetSessionEmbedUrl` API action. Once you have the URL, you can use `embedSession(options)` from the **QuickSight Embedding SDK** to embed the QuickSight console into your web application. For more information, go to `https://github.com/awslabs/amazon-QuickSight-embedding-sdk`.

Now that we've discussed the two types of embedded analytics, in the next section, we will discuss the embedded analytics architecture.

Exploring the architecture and user authentication

In this section, we will focus on the architectural components of embedded analytics. To understand this end-to-end architecture, we will break it down into three layers:

- Web application layer
- BI and data layer
- Authentication and authorization layer

This is better represented with the following diagram:

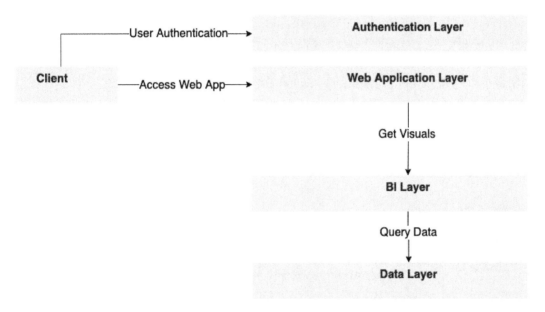

Figure 7.1 – Generic architecture for embedded analytics

Generally, a client typically accesses a web app or a web portal using their web browser. In many cases, the user will need to authenticate with the web app. The client will present user credentials (typically, a username and a password) to the **authentication layer**, which sends back an access code/token so that the client can communicate with the **web application layer**. In embedded analytics, the web application layer will be responsible for getting the embedded visuals from the **BI layer**, which, in turn, would be responsible for querying the data from the data sources and visualizing them (**data layer**).

In the next section, we will analyze each of these architectural components and identify AWS services that can be used to build them.

Overview of the web application layer

In embedded dashboarding applications, embedded dashboards are embedded within this layer. The web application layer interfaces with both the authentication layer and the dashboarding layer. A web application is typically accessed by the user's web browser. The web application layer is responsible for sending the application's content back to the browser user. Ensuring that the web application layer has enough resources to support your users is your responsibility, and you will need to make sure that there is enough capacity for your web server to accept incoming connections. For that reason, you can consider AWS serverless services such as **Amazon Lambda**, **Amazon S3**, for static content, and **Amazon API Gateway** to build a serverless web application that scales automatically to the incoming demand. Other options include the other compute and container services, such as **Amazon EKS**, **ECS**, **Fargate**, and **EC2**. You can also host this layer outside of AWS, which means that you don't need to move your application to the AWS cloud to make use of QuickSight's embedded analytics. For embedded analytics to work, you will need to whitelist the domain of your web application in QuickSight's settings.

To whitelist a domain in Amazon QuickSight, follow these steps:

1. Log in as an admin user and select **Manage QuickSight** from the top right-hand corner's drop-down menu.

2. Next, select **Domains and Embedding** to go to the menu shown in the following screenshot:

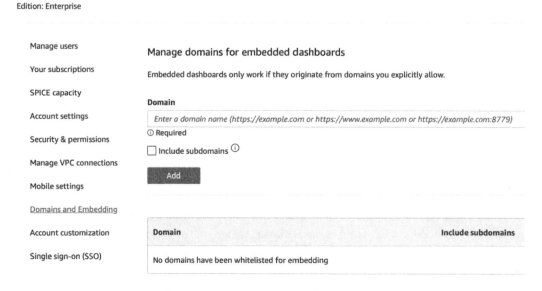

Figure 7.2 – Domains and embedding settings

3. Type in the domain of your web application and click **Add**. Note that you have the option to include subdomains if you need to by simply checking the **Include subdomains** checkbox.

Now that we've discussed the web application layer, we will move on to the BI layer.

Overview of the BI layer

The dashboard layer is the component that serves embedded dashboards to the web application layer. Amazon QuickSight is the central component of this layer. This layer can be embedded too, with the full console embedding. The BI layer is responsible for the following:

- Integrating with data sources
- Enforcing access to dashboards
- Serving embedded dashboard URLs

Concerning scalability, QuickSight will scale automatically for the number of users you configure. If you have anonymous embedding, you will need to enable session capacity planning. This layer interfaces with the data stores, eliminating the need to embed code that accesses the data stores into your application, which simplifies the integration with data sources. To work with datasets, you must use the QuickSight capabilities we learned about in *Chapter 3, Preparing Data with Amazon QuickSight*, rather than developing custom code. Visuals and insights are developed using QuickSight's native capabilities. Finally, at this layer, we configure which users have access to which dashboards. Authorized users get a dashboard URL with an authorization code, while users who don't have access won't get the dashboard URL. Next, we will talk about the authentication layer of an embedded analytics solution within QuickSight.

Understanding the authentication layer

User authorization and authentication are important considerations when building embedded BI applications with QuickSight. The key questions to be addressed are as follows:

- How do you authenticate your users? (Authentication)
- Which users have access to which dashboards? (Authorization)

In embedded analytics, it is common that users authenticate with credentials that are stored outside of Amazon QuickSight in an identity store. You can use **Amazon Cognito** User Pool as an identity store for your cloud-native embedded analytics architecture. You can configure your identity provider with IAM so that you can assume IAM roles for your authenticated entities.

To configure an identity provider with IAM, follow these steps:

1. Log in as an AWS administrator and open the IAM console.

2. Click on the **Identity providers** option, as shown here:

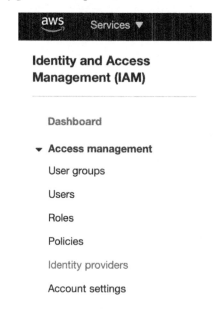

Figure 7.3 – Configuring identity providers

3. Select the type of identity provider (SAML or OIDC) and provide the required metadata for your identity provider.

Once you have set up the identity provider, you can configure trust relationships for IAM roles. Your web application will need to be able to assume an IAM role that has access to the required QuickSight APIs so that it can retrieve the embedding URLs.

An example policy that allows the caller to call the GetDashboardEmbedUrl and GetAuthCode functions for all resources is shown here:

```
{
    "Version": "2012-10-17",
    "Statement": [
```

```
{
    "Sid": "VisualEditor0",
    "Effect": "Allow",
    "Action": [
        "QuickSight:GetDashboardEmbedUrl",
        "QuickSight:GetAuthCode"
    ],
    "Resource": "*"
}
]
}
```

Policies can be assigned to IAM roles, which can be assumed by applications before they call AWS services. A policy will determine the level of access to AWS. The next important step is to establish a trust relationship between the IAM identity provider and the role so that authenticated entities can assume the role and generate the embedding dashboard URL. When you create an IAM role, you will need to select the type of trusted entity. The choice is between an AWS service, such as a role that can be assumed by a service, for example, AWS Lambda, another AWS account, a web identity such as Amazon Cognito or other OpenID identity providers, or SAML 2.0 Federation for corporate users. You will see the following when selecting the type of your entity when creating a role:

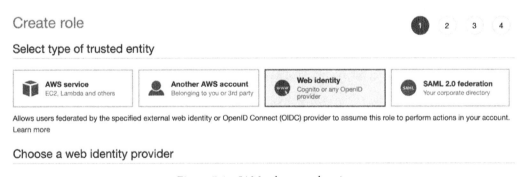

Figure 7.4 – IAM role trusted entity

Once you create the role, you can attach a policy with the required permissions to call the QuickSight APIs for the dashboard embedding. To get the temporary credentials, your web application layer will need to call the **Amazon STS** service's AssumeRole API or AssumeRoleWithSAML or AssumeRoleWithWebIdentity, depending on the identity provider. Once you have the required credentials, then your web application will be able to call the QuickSight APIs to retrieve the embed URL, which is then added to your web frontend.

Now that we have seen the main functionality of the three main architectural components, in the next section, we will describe the E2E flow of embedded analytics.

Putting everything together

Now that we have looked at the main architectural components of the architecture, we will enrich *Figure 7.1* by adding more specific components (including the relevant AWS services) to each of its layers.

For the authentication layer, we can use the following AWS services:

- **IAM** to define your required roles
- A **Cognito** User Pool or another compliant IDP as the identity provider

For the web application layer, we can use the following services:

- AWS **Lambda, S3**, and **API Gateway**. There are several examples online of how to use these services to build a serverless web application using these services.
- Other options include hosting our web app using **container** services or using Amazon **EC2** instances. You are not limited to hosting your web application on AWS; you can host your web application anywhere, including on-premises if you need to.

For the BI layer, we can use the following service:

- **Amazon QuickSight**, including its SPICE storage

For the data layer, we can use the following services:

- **Amazon S3** as the central data lake storage.
- **Amazon Athena**, which allows you to perform SQL queries over data stored in S3 or other data stores (using Federated Query: `https://docs.aws.amazon.com/athena/latest/ug/connect-to-a-data-source.html`).
- **Amazon Redshift** as a data warehouse. **Snowflake**, another popular cloud data warehouse, is also natively supported.
- Other databases that are hosted inside or outside AWS.

After adding these components, our architecture diagram will look as follows:

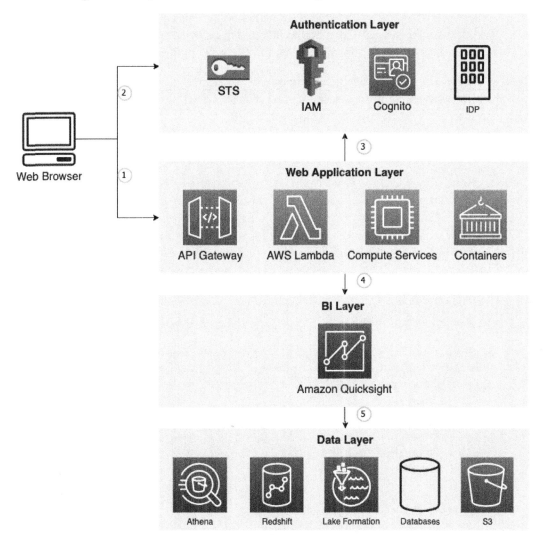

Figure 7.5 – Dashboard embedding with AWS services

The flow for dashboard embedding would be as follows:

1. The user uses their web browser to open the web portal application.

2. The user authenticates with the identity provider and accesses the resource provider via the web application.

3. The web application assumes the embedding **IAM** role.

4. Using the IAM role, the web server calls QuickSight APIs to get the embed URL and display it to the user.

5. To populate the visuals, QuickSight will fetch the data from the various data sources, abstracting this from the user and the web application.

Now that we have explored the main components of the embedded analytics architecture and the flow between components, in the next section, we will use a few simple commands to generate an embedded dashboard URL.

Generating an embedded dashboard URL

In this section, we will use the QuickSight CLI to generate an embedded dashboard URL that, for this example, we will display on a web browser. Setting up authentication and the web server is outside the scope of this book. In *Chapter 2, Introduction to Amazon QuickSight*, we created a reader user in our QuickSight account. First, let's verify the details of this user and get their unique resource number:

1. Log in to the AWS console as a QuickSight or AWS admin and open **AWS CloudShell**.

2. To view the details of the reader user, use the describe-user CLI command:

```
$aws quicksight describe-user --user-name reader
--aws-account-id <aws account id> --namespace default
--region us-east-1
```

Verify that the user has been found. The response should look similar to the following:

```
{
    "Status": 200,
    "User": {
        "Arn": "arn:aws:quicksight:us-east-1:<aws account
id>:user/default/reader",
        "UserName": "reader",
        "Email": "your-email@something.com",
        "Role": "READER",
        "IdentityType": "QUICKSIGHT",
        "Active": true,
        "PrincipalId": ""
    },
    "RequestId": "818a21fc-4146-3bf6-b5c3-a1b315cb874b"
}
```

Note the User Arn property as we will use it later in *Step 4*.

3. Next, we will need to retrieve our dashboard ID. We will use the list-dashboards CLI command to do. Type in the following command. Replace <aws account id> with the 12-digit long ID from your AWS account. Ensure your dashboard is shared with the admin user so that the following command returns the expected results:

```
$aws quicksight list-dashboards --aws-account-id <aws
account id> --region us-east-1
```

So far, we have only created one dashboard, so the response should look as follows:

```
{
    "DashboardSummaryList": [
        {
            "Arn": "arn:aws:QuickSight:us-east-1:<aws
account id>:dashboard/<dashboard id>",
            "DashboardId": "<dashboard id>",
            "Name": "New York Taxi Dashboard",
            "CreatedTime": "2021-06-
02T19:19:00.285000+00:00",
            "LastUpdatedTime": "2021-07-
06T22:55:04.960000+00:00",
            "PublishedVersionNumber": 14,
            "LastPublishedTime": "2021-06-
02T19:19:00.285000+00:00"
        }
    ],
    "Status": 200,
    "RequestId": ""
}
```

Note the dashboard ID as we will use it in the next step.

4. Next, we will use the get-dashboard-embed-url CLI command to generate the embedding URL. Type the following command. Replace the AWS account ID with your 12-digit long account ID, along with the dashboard ID we captured in *Step 3*, and the user arn property that we captured in *Step 1*:

```
%aws quicksight get-dashboard-embed-url --aws-account-id
<aws account id> --dashboard-id <dashboard id>
--identity-type QUICKSIGHT --user-arn <user arn> --region
us-east-1
```

This command will return the following output:

```
{
    "Status": 200,
    "EmbedUrl": "https://us-east-1. quicksight.aws.
amazon.com/embed/xxxxxxxxxx/dashboards/xxxxx-xxxx-xxxx-
xxxx-xxxxxxxx?code=xxxxxxxxxxxxxxxxxxxxxxxxxxxxxxxxxxxxxx
xxxxxxxx
&identityprovider=QuickSight&xisauthcode=true",
    "RequestId":  "xxxxxx-xxxx-xxxxx-xxxxx-xxxxx"
}
```

Note the EmbedUrl value. For this example, just open a browser and paste the embed URL to view the dashboard. This will look as follows:

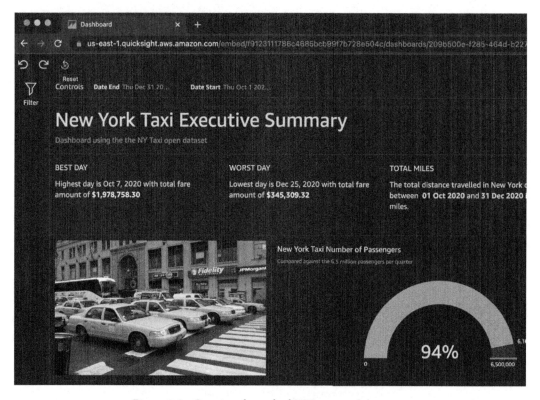

Figure 7.6 – Opening the embed URL on a web browser

In real-world examples, the embed URL will be generated by your application server, and the embed URL will be embedded within your web server. The domain of your web server will need to be whitelisted.

Summary

Congratulations on completing this chapter. In this chapter, we learned about the embedding capabilities of Amazon QuickSight and talked about the different types of embedded analytics. We started by focusing on its main drivers and business benefits. We learned about the main architectural components of dashboard embedding, and then we identified key AWS services that can be used to build these architectural layers. We discussed the end-to-end flow of embedded analytics. Finally, we used simple CLI commands to generate a read-only dashboard URL so that we could see the APIs in action.

In the next chapter, we will focus on managing QuickSight and learn how to automate operations using the QuickSight API.

Q&A

Answer the following questions to test your knowledge of this chapter:

1. What are the main drivers for dashboard embedding?

2. What are the different types of embedded analytics with Amazon QuickSight?

3. What is the role of the STS service in the embedded analytics flow?

4. What is session capacity planning and what type of embedded analytics is relevant to it?

5. What are the different layers in the embedded analytics architecture?

Further reading

For more information on the topics that were covered in this chapter, take a look at the following resources:

- *QuickSight User Guide* – AWS: https://docs.aws.amazon.com/QuickSight/latest/user/amazon-QuickSight-user.pdf

- *Working with Embedded Analytics* – AWS: https://docs.aws.amazon.com/QuickSight/latest/user/embedded-analytics.html

- *Build Your First Serverless Web Application* – AWS: https://aws.amazon.com/serverless/build-a-web-app/

Section 3: Advanced Topics and Management

This chapter will focus on managing and monitoring Amazon QuickSight using the QuickSight API and other AWS services, such as Amazon CloudTrail. We will also look at multitenancy with namespaces.

This section consists of the following chapters:

- *Chapter 8, Understanding the QuickSight API*
- *Chapter 9, Managing QuickSight Permissions and Usage*
- *Chapter 10, Multitenancy in Amazon QuickSight*

8

Understanding the QuickSight API

In this chapter, we will learn how to perform operations using the **Amazon QuickSight** API. We will also explore patterns to automate dataset operations, and we'll demonstrate some of the API actions that allow us to control our account settings. After completing this chapter, you will be familiar with the QuickSight API and how to programmatically control its resources, which is essential when building automation.

We will cover the following topics in this chapter:

- Introducing the QuickSight API
- Controlling resources using the API

Technical requirements

For this chapter, you will need access to the following:

- An **AWS account** and an **AWS Identity and Access Management (IAM)** user, with elevated access
- **Python 3**

- An Amazon QuickSight account with Author and Reader users configured
- The environment created in *Chapter 1, Introducing the AWS Analytics Ecosystem*
- The dashboards created in *Chapter 3, Preparing Data with Amazon QuickSight*

Introducing the QuickSight API

In this section, we will introduce the Amazon QuickSight API. An **application programming interface** (**API**) is a set of defined functions that allow application developers to access the features of a certain application or library. The AWS API allows developers to access AWS services programmatically. Traditionally, AWS provided infrastructure services, allowing developers to programmatically provision virtual machines on the cloud. Now, AWS provides many more services, many of which are not infrastructure services. Amazon QuickSight is a great example of one such service. QuickSight is a cloud-based **business intelligence** (**BI**) service that runs on AWS infrastructure, but developers don't need to provision infrastructure. Instead, developers can use the QuickSight API to access features and conduct actions in the application, such as creating datasets, performing data analysis, or sharing dashboards. So far in this book, we have learned how to complete these operations using the QuickSight console with a **graphical user interface** (**GUI**) accessed via a web browser. In this chapter, we will learn how to complete these operations programmatically, which will allow us to build automation when creating BI applications. First, we will learn how to access the QuickSight API.

Accessing the QuickSight API

In this section, we will learn about the methods you can use to access the QuickSight API. There are two main ways of accessing AWS APIs:

- Using a **software development kit** (**SDK**)
- Using the **command-line interface** (**CLI**)

Next, we will look at these options in more detail with hands-on examples.

Accessing the QuickSight API using the AWS CLI

AWS provides a simple CLI that allows developers to access the AWS API. Before using the CLI, you will need to install it. Follow the AWS instructions to install the CLI for your operating system:

```
https://docs.aws.amazon.com/cli/latest/userguide/cli-chap-
install.html
```

Verifying the installation

Once installed, open a terminal and run the following command to check what CLI version was installed:

```
$aws -version
aws-cli/2.1.13 Python/3.7.4 Darwin/20.5.0 exe/x86_64 prompt/off
```

Configuring the AWS CLI

Now that we have installed the CLI, we need to configure it. First, we need to create a set of credentials that will be used by the CLI:

1. Log in to the AWS Console with your user credentials.

2. Open **Services** and select **Identity and Access Manager**.

3. Under **Access Management**, select **Users**, and then click on the IAM username whose security credentials need to be generated.

4. On the next page, select the **Security credentials** tab.

Figure 8.1 – Creating access keys

5. Under the **Access keys** section, select **Create access key**.

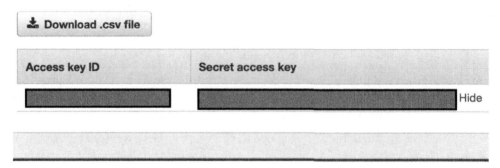

Figure 8.2 – Retrieving the access key

6. Note the values in the **Access key ID** and **Secret access key** fields.

7. Next, open the terminal, run the following command, and add your access key ID and secret access key when prompted. Leave everything else as-is by hitting the *Return* key.

```
$aws configure
```

Accessing the QuickSight API using the CLI

Now that we have configured the CLI, we can run a few commands:

1. To get a list of all QuickSight CLI commands, type the following:

```
$aws quicksight help
```

2. To list our dashboards, type the following command:

```
$ aws quicksight list-dashboards --aws-account-id
<numerical account id> --region us-east-1
{
    "Status": 200,
    "DashboardSummaryList": [
        {
            "Arn": "arn:aws:quicksight:us-east-
1:xxxxxxx:dashboard/xxxxxxxx",
            "DashboardId": "xxxxxxx",
            "Name": "New York Taxi Dashboard",
            "CreatedTime": "2021-06-
02T20:19:00.285000+01:00",
```

```
                "LastUpdatedTime": "2021-07-
    06T23:55:04.960000+01:00",
                "PublishedVersionNumber": 14,
                "LastPublishedTime": "2021-06-
    02T20:19:00.285000+01:00"
            }
        ],
        "RequestId": "xxxxxxx"
    }
```

Note the structure of the CLI command:

- `aws`: To access all CLI commands.

- `quicksight`: To access the QuickSight CLI commands.

- `list-dashboards`: To access the API that returns all the dashboards for an account and region.

- Options (`--`): Use this symbol to add options for the command.

Now that we have configured the CLI and run a simple command, feel free to experiment with the other commands before proceeding to the next section. Refer to the AWS documentation to view the available and required options for your selected CLI command:

`https://awscli.amazonaws.com/v2/documentation/api/latest/reference/quicksight/index.html`

Next, we will access the QuickSight API using the **AWS SDK**.

Accessing the QuickSight API using SDKs

AWS provides various development kits that support a number of programming languages. This means developers can integrate their applications with AWS services without the need to change their programming language. Most common programming languages are supported by AWS, including **Python**, **Java**, **C++**, **Go**, **JavaScript**, and **Ruby**. For more information on the latest language support, refer to the AWS documentation at `https://aws.amazon.com/tools/`. To better understand the AWS SDK, we will use a simple hands-on example. For this example, we will use the Python SDK to programmatically retrieve the QuickSight dashboards and print their names on the screen.

Installing the AWS SDK

For this example, we will use the Python AWS SDK. You will need to install Python in your environment if you haven't already.

If you have Python installed, then type the following command in a terminal:

```
$pip install boto3
```

Next, open your preferred code editor, and type in the upcoming Python code.

> **Note**
> AWS provides a cloud-based **integrated development environment (IDE)**, called **Cloud9**.

To create a Cloud9 environment, log in to the AWS Console and select **Cloud9** from the services list. For this tutorial, you can leave all the default settings as they are. For more information on setting up Cloud9, follow the AWS documentation:

https://docs.aws.amazon.com/cloud9/latest/user-guide/create-environment.html

Before running the following code, replace the AwsAccountId value with the numerical account ID from your environment:

```
import boto3

client = boto3.client('quicksight',region_name='us-east-1')

response = client.list_dashboards(AwsAccountId='xxxxxxxxx')
dashboards_list = response['DashboardSummaryList']
print('Number of dashboards: ' + str(len(dashboards_list)) + '\n')
for dashboard in dashboards_list:
    print(dashboard['Name'])
```

Save the Python script and run it. It should print the total number of dashboards for that region, followed by the name of each dashboard.

Controlling resources using the QuickSight API

In this section, we will learn how to control QuickSight resources using the QuickSight API. This section is not meant to be a full reference guide to the QuickSight API, nor is it going to cover every possible action that can be done using the API. For a full reference guide to the QuickSight API, please refer to the QuickSight documentation:

```
https://docs.aws.amazon.com/quicksight/latest/APIReference/
Welcome.html
```

This section will provide you with practical hands-on examples of using the API to control QuickSight resources. These examples will give you a solid understanding of the types of activities that can be completed using the API, which in turn will help you to manage your QuickSight environment.

Our first example will be to learn how to set up a data source using the QuickSight API.

Setting up a dataset using the CLI

In *Chapter 2, Introduction to Amazon QuickSight*, we learned how to create data sources and datasets. To create these resources, we accessed the QuickSight GUI via our web browser. While the GUI is user-friendly, we can create datasets programmatically using the API. This can be a good option when we need to ensure the consistency of a specific configuration, as manual configurations can be prone to errors. Let's create a data source from the data warehouse we created in *Chapter 1, Introducing the AWS Analytics Ecosystem*.

> **Note**
>
> The tutorial from *Chapter 1, Introducing the AWS Analytics Ecosystem*, included creating a sample **Amazon Redshift** cluster, which will incur charges. For this tutorial, you don't need the cluster running. A paused cluster can work well for this example, as we only need to configure the dataset and we won't need a live connection to it.

Now, let's create a Redshift data source using the CLI. We will use the `create-data-source` CLI command to create a Redshift data source:

```
https://docs.aws.amazon.com/cli/latest/reference/quicksight/
create-data-source.html
```

Here are a few parameters we need to configure:

- `AwsAccountId`: This value represents your AWS numerical account ID.

- `DataSourceId` and `Name`: You will need to define a unique account and region identifier and a user-friendly name to describe your data source.

- `Type`: This is the type of data source. For Redshift data sources, this needs to be set up as `REDSHIFT`.

- `DataSourceParameters`: The type of data source parameters will depend on the type of data source you configure. For Redshift data sources, you will need to define the hostname, port number, Redshift database name, and cluster identifier.

- `Credentials`: These are the credentials required by QuickSight to access the data store. For Redshift data sources, you can use a credential pair consisting of a username and password.

- `Permissions`: In this section, you will need to define the permissions for the newly created datasets and determine which user has access to it and what levels of access they have. For our example, we want our reader user to be able to create datasets from the newly created data source, but we also want to restrict that user from deleting or updating the data source.

Now, let's see how to configure the Redshift connection described previously, using the QuickSight CLI:

1. First, open a text editor and copy the following **JSON** configuration. Replace the highlighted values with those from your environment. For the permissions, note that we only give permissions to the `PassDataSource`, `DescribeDataSource`, and `DescribeDataSourcePermissions` actions, which will allow this user to use this data source to set up new datasets, but it will not allow them to update or delete the data source:

```
{
    "AwsAccountId": "<account id>",
    "DataSourceId": "RedshiftDatasouceCLI",
    "Name": "CLI Datasouce",
    "Type": "REDSHIFT",
    "DataSourceParameters": {
        "RedshiftParameters": {
            "Host": "hostname",
            "Port": 5439,
```

```
                "Database": "dev",
                "ClusterId": "mycluster"
            }
        },
        "Credentials": {
            "CredentialPair": {
                "Username": "admin",
                "Password": "R3dsh1ft"
            }
        },
        "Permissions": [
            {
                "Principal": "arn:aws:quicksight:us-east-
1:xxxxxxxxxxx:user/default/author",
                "Actions": [
                    "quicksight:DescribeDataSource",

  "quicksight:DescribeDataSourcePermissions",
                    "quicksight:PassDataSource"
                ]
            }
        ]
}
```

2. Save the file as `create-data-source.json`.

3. Run `aws quicksight create-data-source --cli-input-json file://create-data-source.json`.

The result of this command will look like the following:

```
{
    "Status": 202,
    "DataSourceId": "SampleRedshiftDatasouce",
    "RequestId": "xxxxxx-xxxxx-xxxxx-xxxxx-xxxxxxxxxx",
    "CreationStatus": "CREATION_IN_PROGRESS",
    "Arn": "arn:aws:quicksight:us-east-
1:xxxxxxxxxxx:datasource/SampleRedshiftDatasouce"
}
```

Now that we have configured the new data source, let's validate that the Author user will be able to use it to set up a new dataset:

1. For this tutorial, we can verify the newly created data source simply by logging into QuickSight as the `author` user.

2. Then, navigate to **Datasets**, and then click **New Datasets**. You should be able to find the newly created data source under the **FROM EXISTING DATA SOURCES** menu, as shown in the following figure:

Figure 8.3 – Creating a data source using the CLI

3. Click on the data source. Note that the buttons to delete or edit the data source are not shown, as this user doesn't have the permissions required to update or delete this data source:

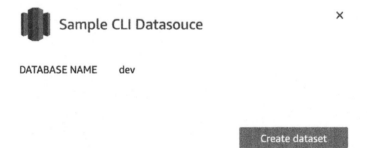

Figure 8.4 – Sample CLI data source permissions

Now that we have learned how to configure a data source, we will use the QuickSight CLI to change the QuickSight settings for our environment.

Editing account settings using the QuickSight API

In this section, we will use the QuickSight API to edit settings on our account. This allows us to configure account customizations on our account. For our example, we will change the default theme for our QuickSight Account.

1. First, let's use the QuickSight API to retrieve the global QuickSight account details. Using the CLI as a QuickSight or AWS admin, type the following command, replacing the `aws-account-id` value with the value from your environment:

```
$aws quicksight describe-account-settings
--aws-account-id <account-id>
```

The response should look like the following:

```
{
    "Status": 200,
    "AccountSettings": {
        "DefaultNamespace": "default",
        "Edition": "ENTERPRISE",
        "NotificationEmail": "your-email",
        "AccountName": "quicksight-account-name"
    },
    "RequestId": "xxxxxxxxxxxxxxxxxxxxxxxx"
}
```

2. Next, let's type the following command to get our QuickSight account customizations. *Account customizations* refer to a set of settings that can be parameterized for a QuickSight account. Currently, you can add a custom default theme by using account customization:

```
$aws quicksight describe-account-customization
--aws-account-id <account-id>
```

Since we haven't yet added any customizations, the response would most likely look like the following:

```
An error occurred (ResourceNotFoundException) when
calling the DescribeAccountCustomization operation:
Account customization does not exist for AwsAccountId
<account-id>
```

3. Now, let's add an account customization and set `Midnight` as the default theme. Type the following command using the CLI, replacing the `aws-account-id` value with your account ID value:

```
aws quicksight create-account-customization
--aws-account-id <account-id> --account-customization
DefaultTheme=arn:aws:quicksight::aws:theme/MIDNIGHT
--region=us-east-1
```

4. Now, let's confirm the creation of the new account customization by running again the `describe-account-customization` command from *Step 2*. This time, the response should look like the following:

```
{
    "Status": 200,
    "RequestId":  "xxxxxx-xxxx-xxxx-xxxx-xxxxxxxxxxx",
    "AccountCustomization": {
        "DefaultTheme": "arn:aws:quicksight::aws:theme/
MIDNIGHT"
    },
    "Arn": "arn:aws:quicksight:us-east-
1:xxxxxxxxxxxx:customization/account/xxxxxxxxxxxx ",
    "AwsAccountId": "xxxxxxxxxxxx "
}
```

> **Note**
>
> The account customization applies at the account and **AWS Region** levels.

To verify that the customization setting has been applied on this account, you can create a sample analysis on the account for the same region where you applied the account customization.

Now that we have learned how to edit our account settings using the CLI, in the next section, we will learn how to use the template API, which is useful when developing analysis and dashboards across multiple environments.

Reusing assets using the template API

QuickSight offers a template API, which allows you to build blueprints for analysis and then use those blueprints to create other analyses for different users, or even for different accounts, with consistency. Templates are not visible on the GUI, and we can access them only by using the API. Next, we will show a simple example of creating a template using the New York Taxi analysis:

1. First, let's list our existing analysis. Using the CLI, type the following command, replacing the `<account-id>` value with the value from your account:

    ```
    $aws quicksight list-analyses --aws-account-id
    <account-id> --region us-east-1
    ```

    Note the `analysis-id` value from our New York Taxi analysis.

2. Next, we will capture additional analysis details, including details about our datasets. Type the following command, replacing the `<account-id>` and `analysis-id` values with the values from your environment:

    ```
    aws quicksight describe-analysis --aws-account-id
    <account-id> --analysis-id xxxxxxx-xxxx-xxxxx-xxxxx-
    xxxxxxxxxx --region us-east-1
    ```

    The response should look like this:

    ```
    {
        "Status": 200,
        "Analysis": {
            "Status": "CREATION_SUCCESSFUL",
            "Name": "yellowtrips_3mo analysis",
            "LastUpdatedTime": 1629144517.0,
            "DataSetArns": [
                "arn:aws:quicksight:us-east-1:
    xxxxxxxxxxxx:dataset/xxxxxxx-xxxx-xxxxx-xxxxx-
    xxxxxxxxxx",
                "arn:aws:quicksight:us-east-1:
    xxxxxxxxxxxx:dataset/xxxxxxx-xxxx-xxxxx-xxxxx-xxxxxxxxxx
    "
            ],
            "CreatedTime": 1621766161.633,
            "Sheets": [
                {
    ```

```
                    "SheetId": " xxxxxxx-xxxx-xxxxx-xxxxx-
xxxxxxxxxx ",
                    "Name": "Executive Summary"
            }
        ],
        "ThemeArn": "arn:aws:quicksight::aws:theme/
MIDNIGHT",
        "Arn": "arn:aws:quicksight:us-east-1:
xxxxxxxxxxxx:analysis/xxxxxxx-xxxx-xxxxx-xxxxx-
xxxxxxxxxx",
        "AnalysisId": "xxxxxxx-xxxx-xxxxx-xxxxx-
xxxxxxxxxx"
    },
    "RequestId": " xxxxxxx-xxxx-xxxxx-xxxxx-xxxxxxxxxx "
}
```

Capture the dataset's `arn` value (highlighted), as we will use them in the next step.

3. Next, open a text editor and paste the following JSON configuration, which will be used to create our first QuickSight template. Replace the `AwsAccountId`, source analysis `arn`, and dataset references `arn` values with the values from your environment. Save the file as `create-template.json`:

```
{
    "AwsAccountId": "xxxxxxxxxxxx",
    "TemplateId": "first-template",
    "Name": "My First Template",
    "SourceEntity": {
        "SourceAnalysis": {
            "Arn": "arn:aws:quicksight:us-east-1:
xxxxxxxxxxxx:analysis/xxxxxxx-xxxx-xxxxx-xxxxx-
xxxxxxxxxx",
            "DataSetReferences": [
                {
                    "DataSetPlaceholder": "Main Dataset",
                    "DataSetArn": "arn:aws:quicksight:us-
east-1: xxxxxxxxxxxx:dataset/xxxxxxx-xxxx-xxxxx-xxxxx-
xxxxxxxxxx"
                },
```

```
                    {
                        "DataSetPlaceholder": "Enrich
Dataset",
                        "DataSetArn": "arn:aws:quicksight:us-
east-1: xxxxxxxxxxxx:dataset/xxxxxxx-xxxx-xxxxx-xxxxx-
xxxxxxxxxx"
                    }
                ]
            }
        },
        "VersionDescription": "1"
    }
```

4. Next, we will confirm the creation of our template. As mentioned earlier, a template can only be used and listed using the QuickSight API, and there isn't a UI element to it. Using the CLI, we will type the following command:

```
$aws quicksight list-templates --aws-account-id
<account-id> --region us-east-1
```

The response should look like this:

```
{
    "Status": 200,
    "TemplateSummaryList": [
        {
            "LatestVersionNumber": 1,
            "LastUpdatedTime": 1629320961.782,
            "TemplateId": "first-template",
            "CreatedTime": 1629320961.782,
            "Arn": "arn:aws:quicksight:us-east-
1:xxxxxxxxxxxxxx:template/first-template",
            "Name": "My First Template"
        }
    ],
    "RequestId": "xxxxxxxxxxx"
}
```

5. Next, we will use this template to create a new analysis. For this example, to avoid incurring costs, we will use our existing Author user, and we'll create an analysis from a template. For this part, we'll use the `create-analysis` CLI command. Open a text editor and paste the following, then save it as `create-analysis-from-template.json`. Replace the highlighted values with those matching your environment:

```json
{
    "AwsAccountId": "xxxxxxxxxxx",
    "AnalysisId": "analysis-from-template",
    "Name": "Analysis From Template",
    "Permissions": [
        {
            "Principal": "arn:aws:quicksight:us-east-1:xxxxxxxxxxx:user/default/author",
            "Actions": [
                "quicksight:RestoreAnalysis",
                "quicksight:UpdateAnalysisPermissions",
                "quicksight:DeleteAnalysis",
                "quicksight:DescribeAnalysisPermissions",
                "quicksight:QueryAnalysis",
                "quicksight:DescribeAnalysis",
                "quicksight:UpdateAnalysis"
            ]
        }
    ],
    "SourceEntity": {
        "SourceTemplate": {
            "DataSetReferences": [
                {
                    "DataSetPlaceholder": "Main Dataset",
                    "DataSetArn": "arn:aws:quicksight:us-east-1: xxxxxxxxxxx:dataset/xxxxxxx-xxxx-xxxxx-xxxxx-xxxxxxxxxx"
                },
                {
                    "DataSetPlaceholder": "Enrich Dataset",
```

```
            "DataSetArn": "arn:aws:quicksight:us-
east-1: xxxxxxxxxxxxx:dataset/xxxxxxx-xxxx-xxxxx-xxxxx-
xxxxxxxxxxx"
            }

        ],
            "Arn": "arn:aws:quicksight:us-east-
1:xxxxxxxxxxx:template/first-template"
        }
      }
  }
```

6. Next, type the following command:

```
$aws quicksight create-analysis --cli-input-json file://
create-analysis-from-template.json --region us-east-1
```

7. You can confirm the creation of the analysis by using the `list-analyses` CLI command:

```
$aws quicksight list-analyses --aws-account-id
xxxxxxxxxxxxx
```

8. Log back into the QuickSight UI as the Author user and view the newly created analysis:

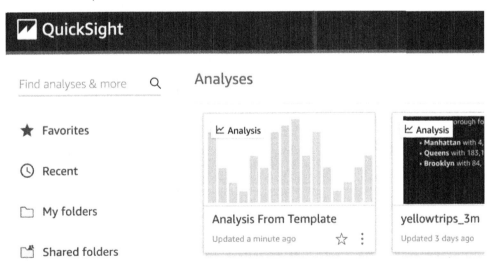

Figure 8.5 – Generating an analysis from a template

Once you open the analysis, you will notice an identical analysis to the one we created in previous chapters. The main difference is that the analysis from the template was created programmatically using a few CLI commands. Using the template and analysis API, we can create and share a blueprint of an analysis, and then using this blueprint, we can create a new analysis and share it with other users or accounts. Without the template API, you would need to recreate the analysis manually, which can involve many steps and makes it harder to apply changes consistently.

Now that we have learned how to control QuickSight resources programmatically, in the next section, we will discuss patterns to build automations.

Building automation using the QuickSight API

So far, we have learned how to use the QuickSight API to control resources by using the AWS CLI. In this section, we will discuss an architecture that will allow us to call the QuickSight API automatically.

Understanding the role of AWS Lambda

AWS Lambda is a serverless compute service that allows you to run code without creating servers. The unit of computation is a *Lambda function*. Lambda functions can be triggered by specific events or at a specific point in time. Using AWS Lambda and the AWS SDK, we can control QuickSight resources programmatically to respond to specific events or changes to our infrastructure. For example, instead of scheduling a refresh on an interval, we could use the SDK to set our data to refresh on specific events.

Amazon EventBridge can be used for more complex integrations. Amazon EventBridge is a serverless event bus that makes it easier to build event-driven applications on AWS. Using EventBridge, you can deliver real-time events that are generated by your applications, integrated **software-as-a-service (SaaS)** applications, and AWS services. AWS Lambda can be a target of these events, and this allows you to design responses to certain events. To better understand how to automate QuickSight operations, in the next section, we will create a simple event-driven ingestion from an **Amazon S3** data source using AWS Lambda.

Automating the ingestion of an Amazon S3 data source

In this section, we will configure a simple application that will automatically refresh an **Amazon SPICE** data source when the underlying S3 data is updated. With this approach, instead of waiting for a scheduled refresh (which would introduce delays), we will trigger a refresh as soon as new data is available (which will minimize delays). For this example, we will use a sample .csv file, which will be configured as an S3 data source in QuickSight. Then, we will configure a Lambda function that will be triggered by S3 notifications. The Lambda function will call the `createIngestion` function of the QuickSight API, which will result in QuickSight importing the new dataset into SPICE. The following figure shows how the various components work together:

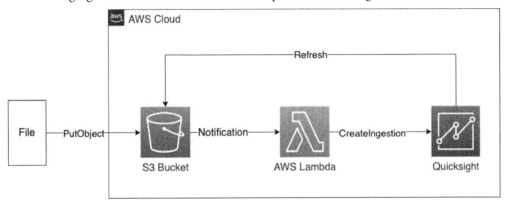

Figure 8.6 – An event-driven data refresh

Now that we have discussed the high-level architecture, to better understand it, let's explore a hands-on example.

Creating an S3 dataset

Let's begin by creating a sample dataset. We will need to create a .csv file and a manifest file:

1. First, open a text editor and create a `sample.csv` file. Copy the following as its content:

    ```
    "Name","Age"
    "George","54"
    ```

2. Upload the file into the S3 data lake you created in *Chapter 1, Introducing the AWS Analytics Ecosystem*. Create a folder named `samples` under your data lake bucket, or simply use the `s3 cp` CLI command to upload your .csv file:

    ```
    $aws s3 cp sample.csv s3://<data-lake-xxxxxxxx>/samples/
    ```

3. Next, we will create a manifest file, which defines which files need to be imported into QuickSight. We can have more than one file, but in this example and for simplicity, we will import a single file. Open a text editor and create a `manifest.json` file. Copy the following, replacing the highlighted values with the values from your environment:

```
{
      "fileLocations": [
          {
              "URIs": [
                  "s3://data-lake-xxxxxxxxx/samples/
sample.csv"
              ]
          }
      ]
}
```

4. Next, we will create an S3 data source in QuickSight. Log in to QuickSight as an Author user and click **Datasets,** and then click **Create**. Select S3 from the list of available sources. Next, name your data source, and upload the manifest file.

5. Once imported, you should be able to edit the dataset and verify its content.

Figure 8.7 – Creating an S3 data source

Now that we have configured our S3 data source and imported it into SPICE, in the next section, we will configure the Lambda function that will trigger a SPICE refresh.

Configuring the QuickSight ingestion Lambda function

In this section, we will learn how to configure a Lambda function to trigger a SPICE refresh. The function will call the `createIngestion` QuickSight API call to refresh the sample dataset we created during the previous steps.

Log in to the AWS console and select **AWS Lambda**. In the Lambda console, select **Create function**. Add the following details:

- **Name**: `quicksight-refresh`
- **Runtime**: `Python 3.8`
- **Execution Role**: `Create a new role with basic Lambda permissions`

Leave the remaining options with their default values, and then click **Create function**.

Before we proceed, we need to make sure our lambda function has the required permissions to call the QuickSight API. Select the IAM role for this function, and add a policy that allows access to the following QuickSight API actions:

- `quicksight:CreateIngestion`
- `quicksight:CancelIngestion`
- `quicksight:DeleteDataSource`
- `quicksight:DeleteDataSet`

For this tutorial, you can use the following policy document. Replace the highlighted values with those from your environment:

```
{
    "Version": "2012-10-17",
    "Statement": [
        {
            "Sid": "VisualEditor0",
            "Effect": "Allow",
            "Action": "quicksight:DeleteDataSet",
            "Resource": "arn:aws:quicksight:*:<aws-account-id>:dataset/*"
        },
        {
```

```
            "Sid": "VisualEditor1",
            "Effect": "Allow",
            "Action": [
                "quicksight:CreateIngestion",
                "quicksight:DeleteDataSource",
                "quicksight:CancelIngestion"
            ],
            "Resource": [
                "arn:aws:quicksight:*:<aws-account-
id>:datasource/*",
                "arn:aws:quicksight:*:<aws-account-
id>:dataset/*/ingestion/*"
            ]
        }
    ]
}
```

Now that our Lambda function has access to the required APIs, let's add the Python code. Using the lambda code editor, simply paste the following code. Replace the highlighted values with the values from your environment:

```python
import boto3
import uuid

client = boto3.client('quicksight')

def lambda_handler(event, context):

    response = client.create_ingestion(
    DataSetId='<dataset-id>,
    IngestionId=uuid.uuid4().hex,
    AwsAccountId='<aws-account-id>'
)

    return response
```

After you complete this step, click **Deploy**. We can test our Lambda function and verify that it triggers a refresh. Look for `"IngestionStatus": "INITIALIZED"` in the response to verify the response from the QuickSight API.

Now that we have configured our Lambda functions, in the next section, we will configure our S3 trigger.

Configuring an S3 trigger

In this section, we will configure our S3 trigger. The trigger should only trigger a refresh when we have new objects in the `samples` folders of our data lake:

1. Open the Lambda console and select **Add trigger**.

2. Select the S3 service from the drop-down menu, and then your S3 data lake bucket. Then, configure the following values:

   - **Event type**: `All object create events`
   - **Prefix**: `samples/`
   - **Suffix**: `.csv`

3. Click **Add** to add the new trigger.

Now that we have configured our trigger, in the next section, we will test our application.

Testing the application

To test the application, complete the following steps:

1. Open the `sample.csv` file and add a new line so that it looks like the following:

```
"Name","Age"
"George","54"
"Anna","56"
```

2. Next, we will update the file in S3. You can either use the AWS Console or AWS CLI:

```
$aws s3 cp sample.csv s3://<data-lake-xxxxxxxxx>/samples/
```

3. This should trigger our Lambda function, which in turn will call the API and trigger a refresh. To verify, log in to QuickSight and select **Datasets**. Select the sample dataset and then edit to access the preview mode:

Figure 8.8 – Previewing the imported data

Note the new values in our dataset. QuickSight completed the ingestion, and now the new values are in SPICE, shortly after we updated the file. A key benefit of our event-driven architecture is that we don't need to wait for a scheduled refresh – instead, data is refreshed as soon as we have new values.

Summary

Congratulations on completing this chapter.

In this chapter, we learned the different options of accessing the QuickSight API, including the CLI, and we have seen an example using the Python SDK. Then, using the AWS CLI, we learned how to control our QuickSight resources programmatically. We learned how to create a new data source programmatically, and we also used the QuickSight API to control the account settings (such as changing the default theme of QuickSight). Finally, using a simple example, we learned how to use the template API to create an analysis blueprint, and then how to use the template to create an analysis programmatically.

Using the things you learned in this chapter, you will be able to control QuickSight resources programmatically, which will make it easier to work across multiple environments and securely and consistently apply changes to your QuickSight account. Finally, using a simple hands-on example, we learned how to build an event-driven application that calls the QuickSight API and automatically imports an S3 dataset into SPICE. In the next chapter, we will learn how to manage QuickSight permissions and usage.

Questions

Here are a few questions to revise what we learned in this chapter.

1. What is a QuickSight template?
2. How can we access the QuickSight API?
3. How can we create an analysis from a template?
4. How can you build automation using the QuickSight API?

Further reading

- *Amazon QuickSight User Guide*:

  https://docs.aws.amazon.com/quicksight/latest/user/amazon-quicksight-user.pdf

9
Managing QuickSight Permissions and Usage

In this chapter, we will learn how to manage **Amazon QuickSight** operations and permissions. We will focus on the QuickSight permissions model and learn how to configure fine-grained permissions. We will also learn how to manage and organize QuickSight assets into folders, and how to set up threshold-based alerts and email reports.

We will cover the following topics in this chapter:

- Managing QuickSight permissions
- Managing QuickSight usage

Technical requirements

For this chapter, you will need access to the following:

- An **AWS** account and **AWS Identity and Access Management (IAM)** user, with elevated access

- The **AWS Command Line Interface (CLI)**

- An Amazon QuickSight account with Author and Reader users configured

- The environment created in *Chapter 1, Introducing the AWS Analytics Ecosystem*

- The dashboards created in *Chapter 4, Developing Visuals and Dashboards*

Managing QuickSight permissions

In this section, we will learn how to configure user permissions against QuickSight resources. First, let's introduce the fundamental topics we need to understand when setting up permissions:

- **Principal**: An AWS principal is the user (or group of users) or application that needs to access AWS resources.

- **Action**: Actions define the set of API operations that a principal is allowed or denied. For example, in QuickSight, the `DeleteDataSet` action deletes a dataset. To see a full list of QuickSight actions, refer to the AWS Documentation: `https://docs.aws.amazon.com/service-authorization/latest/reference/list_amazonquicksight.html#amazonquicksight-actions-as-permissions`.

- **Resource**: For most actions, we can narrow down the scope of a policy to a specific resource(s). Typically, a single resource has its own unique **Amazon Resource Number (arn)**.

- **Condition**: AWS allows you to define access based on specific conditions. For example, a condition that gives access to an application from a specific IP address.

When granting AWS permissions, including QuickSight permissions, make sure you follow the **least privilege** security best practice. According to the principle of least privilege, you should only allow users to have access to the specific actions and resources they require.

Using user groups

As the number of users increases and their access patterns become more and more sophisticated, the complexity of configuring their permissions to resources also rises exponentially. In these circumstances, we can use **user groups**. User groups allow you to group users together and then apply permissions at the group level, rather than the individual level, which saves you time and effort. When a user joins a group, they automatically inherit the group permissions. Likewise, when a user leaves the group, then they lose access to the group's resources.

To better understand how to manage groups in Amazon QuickSight, we will use a simple hands-on example:

1. First, let's create a group for the marketing department. Using a terminal with AWS CLI configured and with elevated access, type the following command, replacing the `<account-id>` value with the value from your environment:

    ```
    $aws quicksight create-group --group-name "Marketing"
    --description "Group for the Marketing Department"
    --aws-account-id <account-id> --namespace default
    --region us-east-1
    ```

2. Next, let's add our Reader user to this group. For this purpose, we will use the `create-group-membership` CLI command. Type the following, replacing the highlighted values with those from your environment:

    ```
    $aws quicksight create-group-membership --member-
    name reader --group-name Marketing --aws-account-id
    <account-id> --namespace default --region us-east-1
    ```

3. Next, we will use the QuickSight Console to share a new dashboard with the marketing group, rather than an individual user. Log into QuickSight as the Author user. Open the New York Taxi analysis and publish it as a brand-new dashboard. Give any name to your newly created dashboard.

4. On the next screen, when sharing the dashboard, select the **Marketing** group and share your dashboard, as shown in the following screenshot:

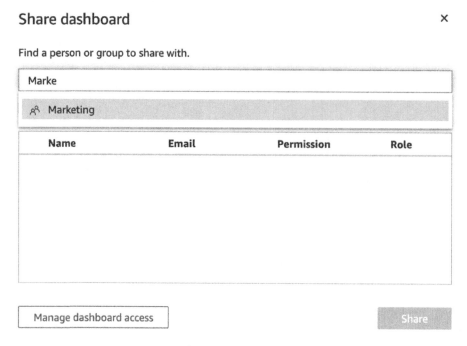

Figure 9.1 – Sharing a dashboard with a group

5. To verify that your dashboard has been shared successfully, log out and log back in as the Reader user. Navigate to **Dashboards**, and notice the newly created dashboard:

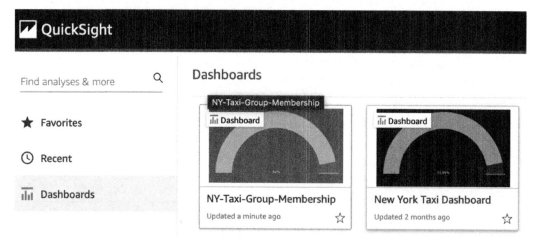

Figure 9.2 – Confirming dashboard group access

Note that we didn't need to give access directly to the Reader user for this dashboard. Instead, we added the Reader user into the **Marketing** group, and then we allowed all users from that group to have access to our published dashboard. In the future, if we had more users joining the **Marketing** group, they would automatically assume access to resources shared with that particular group, eliminating the need to define specific permissions at the individual user level.

Now that we have learned about user groups and how to use them to simplify our permissions, in the next section, we will talk about custom permissions.

Setting up custom permissions

In *Chapter 2, Introduction to Amazon QuickSight*, we learned the different user cohorts: Admin, Author, and Reader. The user cohort determines the level of access to features in the QuickSight console. Custom profiles allow you to override the default permissions with custom security profiles and define permissions that fit your organization's requirements.

> **Note**
> For custom permissions to work, you will need to be using IAM federated users.

To better understand custom permissions, we will use a simple hands-on example. By default, an Author user is able to configure a new data source. For our example, let's assume that to protect our **Amazon SPICE** space, we want to prevent authors from creating new data sources:

1. First, log into the QuickSight Console as a QuickSight Admin user.
2. Expand the QuickSight menu in the top-right corner of the screen and select **Manage QuickSight**.
3. With the **Manage users** option selected, click on **Manage permissions**, as shown in the following screenshot:

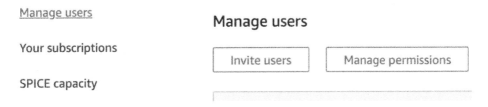

Figure 9.3 – Accessing custom permissions

4. On the next screen, tick the **Creating or updating all data sources** checkbox, as shown in the following screenshot:

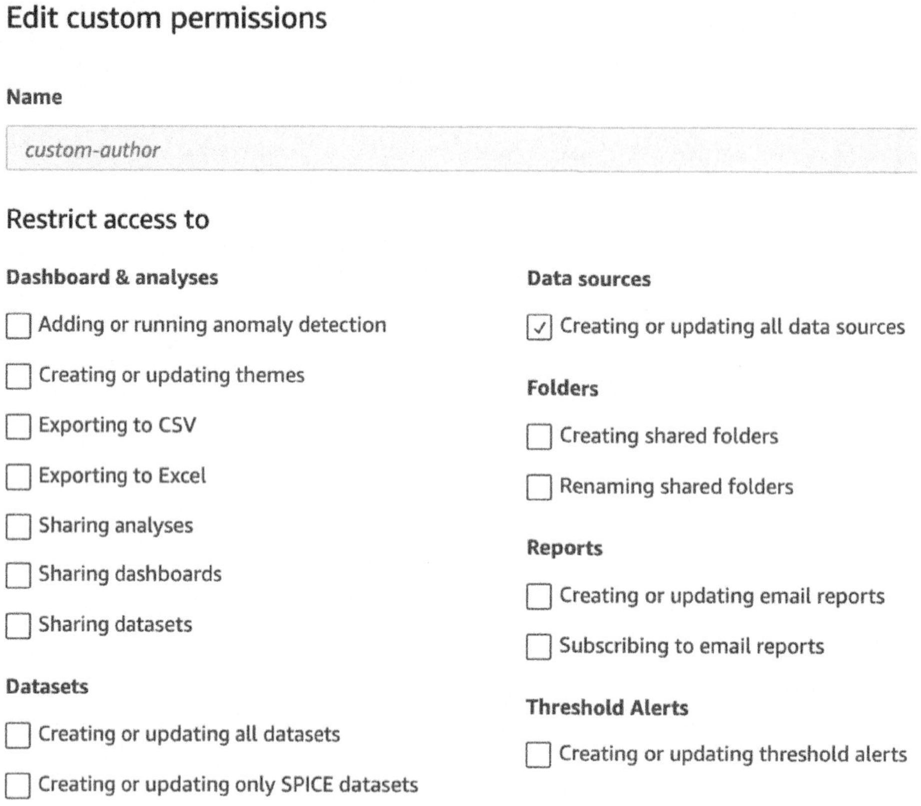

Edit custom permissions

Name

custom-author

Restrict access to

Dashboard & analyses

☐ Adding or running anomaly detection

☐ Creating or updating themes

☐ Exporting to CSV

☐ Exporting to Excel

☐ Sharing analyses

☐ Sharing dashboards

☐ Sharing datasets

Datasets

☐ Creating or updating all datasets

☐ Creating or updating only SPICE datasets

Data sources

☑ Creating or updating all data sources

Folders

☐ Creating shared folders

☐ Renaming shared folders

Reports

☐ Creating or updating email reports

☐ Subscribing to email reports

Threshold Alerts

☐ Creating or updating threshold alerts

Figure 9.4 – Editing custom permissions

> **Note**
>
> When defining custom permissions using the QuickSight Console, you choose which actions you want to *restrict* access to. The rest of the actions will be permitted based on which cohort the user belongs to.

5. Before we assign permissions, it is worth confirming that our Author user will be able to create a new dataset. Log into the QuickSight Console as the Author user and confirm that you can create a new dataset by selecting **New dataset**.

6. Next, we will need to add a new Author user. Make sure you use the IAM credentials for this user by ticking the IAM checkbox when registering the user. For this example, we can call the user author-iam.

7. After you register the new `author-iam` user, we will assign the new custom permissions profile to them. Using the AWS CLI and as the QuickSight Admin user, type the following command, replacing the highlighted values with those from your environment:

```
$aws quicksight update-user --user-name author-iam
--role AUTHOR --custom-permissions-name custom-author
--email <your-email> --aws-account-id <account-id>
--namespace default --region us-east-1
```

8. Now, we have attached our custom permissions to our newly created Author user. We can verify that the console access is as expected. Log out and log back into the QuickSight Console as the `author-iam` user.

9. Next, select **Datasets** from the left-hand side menu, and then select **Create a Dataset**. Your screen should look like the following figure, giving you no options for creating a new dataset:

Figure 9.5 – Applying custom permissions

By applying custom permissions, we were able to override the default Author behavior and prevent our newly registered Author user from creating new data sources. You can configure multiple custom permissions profiles in your QuickSight account and allocate them to your users. A user cannot have more than one custom permissions profile.

10. As a final step, we will deregister the `author-iam` user from QuickSight, since we no longer need them. To deregister the user, you can either use the QuickSight Admin Console or the AWS CLI by typing the following command and replacing the highlighted value with the values from your environment:

```
aws quicksight delete-user --user-name author-iam
--aws-account-id <account-id> --namespace default
--region us-east-1
```

Now that we have learned how to configure custom permissions, in the next section, we will learn how to integrate QuickSight with Amazon Lake Formation.

Integrating with Amazon Lake Formation

In this section, we will learn about the QuickSight integration with Amazon Lake Formation. **Amazon Lake Formation** provides an additional permission layer above the **AWS Glue Data Catalog**, allowing you to set up fine-grained permissions on top of your data lake on AWS. The integration with Lake Formation is useful for **Amazon Athena** datasets. Combined with QuickSight, Lake Formation will allow you to manage your data permissions from a single place, enforcing the permissions at the data lake layer by enhancing the existing QuickSight fine-grained permissions. To understand the value added by Lake Formation, we will first need to understand how to apply permissions for Athena datasets without Lake Formation.

Configuring Amazon Athena datasets permissions without Amazon Lake Formation

To better understand the value of Lake Formation, it is important to understand how to configure permissions for Athena datasets. We will use the demo data we configured in *Chapter 1, Introducing the AWS Analytics Ecosystem*. Specifically, we have configured the following AWS Glue database:

- Database: `my-data-lake-db`
- Table name: `yellowtrips`
- S3 location: `s3://data-lake-xxxxxxxxx/yellowtrips/`

In order to be able to create the Athena dataset, you will need QuickSight to do the following:

- Configure access to Amazon Athena.
- Configure access to the underlying S3 buckets.

In *Chapter 2, Introduction to Amazon QuickSight,* we learned how to give QuickSight access to **Amazon S3** buckets. You can follow a similar process to give access to the Athena service.

To enable Athena access, we can use the following steps:

1. First, log into the AWS Console as the QuickSight Admin user and select **Manage QuickSight**.

2. Select **Security & permissions**.

3. Select **Add or remove** from the QuickSight access to AWS services menu.

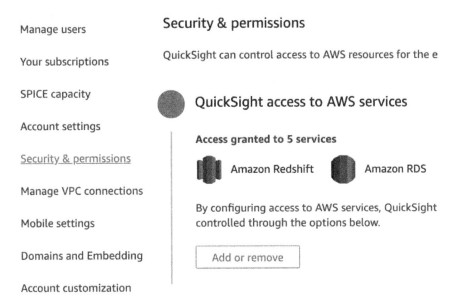

Figure 9.6 – Allowing QuickSight access to other AWS services

4. Select **Athena**, and ensure that the **S3** data lake bucket is also selected.

Amazon Athena resources   ×

S3	Lambda

S3 Buckets Linked To QuickSight Account	S3 Buckets You Can Access Across AWS

Select the buckets that you want QuickSight to be able to access.

Selected buckets have read only permissions by default. However, you must give write permissions for Athena Workgroup feature.

☑ Select all

S3 Bucket	Write permission for Athena Workgroup
☑ data-lake-xxxxxxxxxx	☐

Figure 9.7 – Enabling Amazon Athena access

5.   Click **Finish**.

6.   To verify access, you can create a new Athena dataset (as we learned in *Chapter 2, Introduction to Amazon QuickSight*).

While this is straightforward to set up, it gives all users the same level of access to Athena and S3. It is very common for organizations to have different requirements when it comes to permissions to data for different users and groups. For that reason, QuickSight offers you the ability to define fine-grained access controls. This feature can be accessed via the **Resource access for individual users and groups** menu under the **Security and Permissions** settings. This will allow you to assign specific IAM policies to specific QuickSight users or groups, allowing you to define more detailed permissions to your QuickSight environment.

Now that we have learned how to create Athena datasets without Lake Formation, in the next section, we will understand how to configure datasets that are managed by Lake Formation.

Configuring Amazon Athena datasets with Amazon Lake Formation

Lake Formation provides an additional permission layer over your Athena datasets. Instead of granting permissions using IAM, you register your S3 storage in Lake Formation, and then you can use the Lake Formation Console or the Lake Formation API to grant or revoke permissions to the tables in your data catalog. Lake Formation supports column-based access policies, row-based filtering, and tag-based access controls, which allow you to define advanced and fine-grained access controls for your dataset.

Instead of defining IAM policies and defining assignments to your users or groups, you can use Lake Formation to manage your permissions centrally. In Lake Formation, you manage permissions with a grant/revoke syntax (which will be familiar to **business intelligence** (**BI**) developers), rather than defining **JSON** documents for IAM. When working with QuickSight principals, you will need to use the QuickSight user or group arn as the Lake Formation principal, as shown in the following figure:

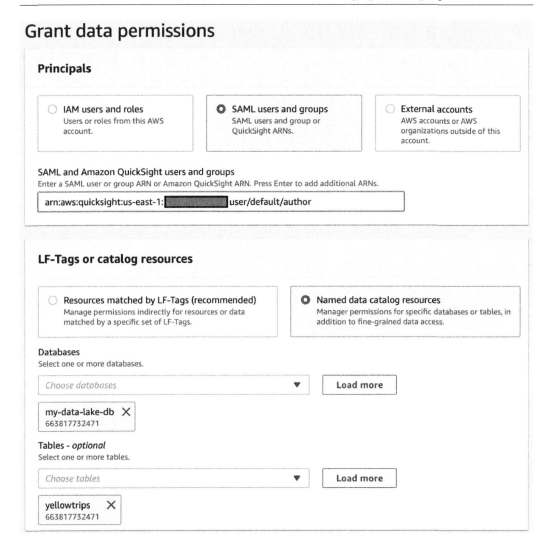

Figure 9.8 – Configuring QuickSight users with Amazon Lake Formation

Defining permissions in Lake Formation allows you to define complex, fine-grained permissions, without writing code or IAM policies. These data permissions are managed centrally within the AWS Console, and this allows you to easily change and verify the level of access each user has for specific datasets.

Now that we have learned how to configure custom permissions and talked briefly about the Lake Formation integration, in the next section, we will learn how to organize QuickSight assets using folders and set up alarms and email reports.

Managing QuickSight usage

In this section, we will focus on managing QuickSight assets. We will learn how to organize QuickSight assets using folders and how to set up alarms and reports.

Managing folders

You can use folders to easily organize, navigate, and discover QuickSight assets. QuickSight *assets* include the following:

- Datasets
- Analyses
- Dashboards

Folders can be either of the following:

- **Personal folders**: These can be used to organize your work for yourself.
- **Shared folders**: These can be used to simplify the sharing of QuickSight assets across multiple teams and BI developers.

> **Note**
>
> Only a QuickSight Admin user can create shared folders. Ownership of shared folders can be transferred to another user who belongs to the Author user cohort. Personal folder ownership always belongs to the user who created it.

To create folders, you can use either the QuickSight Console or QuickSight API. To better understand how to use folders, we will use a hands-on example using the New York Taxi sample dataset, analysis, and dashboard configured in *Chapter 4, Developing Visuals and Dashboards*.

Working with personal folders

In this section, we will work with personal folders and use them to group different assets together. For our example, let's assume that the Author user needs to organize all assets (datasets, analyses, and dashboards) of a specific project together. This will allow them to organize the QuickSight assets as they develop different projects.

To organize these assets, you can use QuickSight folders:

1. First, log into the QuickSight console as the Author user.
2. Then, click **My folders**, and then click **+ New** in the top right-hand corner.

3. Select a meaningful project name for your folder, for example, `New York Taxi Project`.

4. Next, we will add the relevant assets. Locate each asset (dataset, analysis, and dashboard), click **Add to folder**, and select the newly created folder, as shown in the following screenshot:

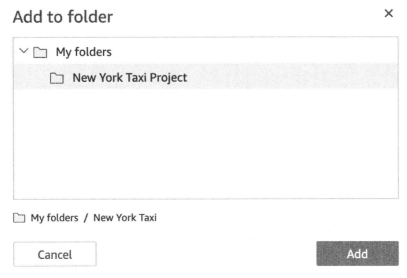

Figure 9.9 – Adding assets to folders

5. After adding all the relevant assets, navigate back to **My folders** and open your `New York Taxi Project` folder, as shown in the following screenshot:

My folders

My folders / New York Taxi Project

	Name	Type		Owner	Last Modified ∨	
	yellowtrips_3mo	Dataset	SPICE	Others	20 hours ago	···
☆	New York Taxi Dashboard	Dashboard		Me	2 months ago	···
☆	yellowtrips_3mo analysis	Analysis		Me	22 days ago	···

Figure 9.10 – Grouping different assets into folders

Note that now we have grouped together different assets relevant to a specific project, which saves you time when searching for relevant assets. The benefits of managing and organizing assets using folders are greater when you have a large number of projects and assets to work with.

Now that we have learned how to use personal folders, in the next section, we will look at shared folders.

Working with shared folders

Shared folders can be used to share assets between users or groups. Shared folders can be particularly useful when there are many BI developers working on a project. You can create shared folders for your users so they can easily find assets in a consistent way. As you onboard new users into your QuickSight environment, you can share folders with the new users, and your users will inherit the access to the underlying assets.

> **Note**
>
> Sharing a folder will give the underlying assets the same permissions as the shared folders. This will allow you to share multiple dashboards that belong to a folder with multiple users or groups, without having to configure specific rules for each asset.

To create a shared folder, we will use the following steps:

1. Log in to the QuickSight Console (or use the CLI) as a QuickSight Admin user and select **Shared folders**, and then select **+ New**.

2. Give your shared folder a meaningful name, and select **Create**.

3. Now we will share our folder with our Reader user. Before this step, to better understand the concept, we will remove the access to the dashboard for that user and then re-enable access by sharing the shared folder, which will contain the dashboard.

4. In *Chapter 4, Developing Visuals and Dashboards*, we learned how to manage user access for QuickSight dashboards. To remove user access from a dashboard, log in as the Author user, open your `New York Taxi` dashboard, then select **Share**, then **Manage Access**, and then remove the Reader user.

5. To add your `New York Taxi` dashboard into your newly created shared folder, simply select the dashboard and select **Add to folder**, as shown in the following screenshot. Select your shared folder, and then click **Add**:

Dashboards

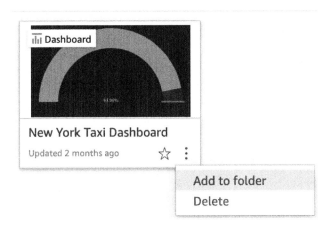

Figure 9.11 – Adding a dashboard to a shared folder

Note the message informing you that your asset will have the same sharing permissions to your shared folder:

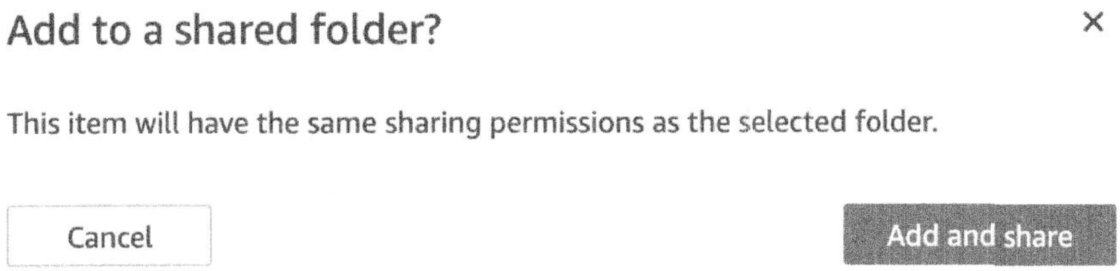

Add to a shared folder?   ×

This item will have the same sharing permissions as the selected folder.

Cancel   Add and share

Figure 9.12 – The sharing permissions message

6. Next, we will share our folder with our Reader user. To share a folder, select the shared folder, and then select **Share** (as shown in the following screenshot), and add your Reader user:

Figure 9.13 – Sharing a folder with other users

7. As a final step, we can verify that the Reader user can open the dashboard shared with them via the shared folder. To verify, log into the QuickSight Console as the Reader user, open the shared folder, and then open your shared dashboard.

Managing folders effectively can help you organize and efficiently share QuickSight assets with your users or group of users. With effective folder management, your users will be able to easily navigate and find the assets they need to view or work with. Access management can also be simplified by grouping assets together in shared folders, and then providing access to the container folder, rather than on an individual asset level.

> **Note**
>
> You can transfer ownership of a shared folder to other QuickSight users who are in the Author or Admin user cohort. Readers cannot own shared folders and can only view them. Reader users can create personal folders only.

Now that we have learned how to work with shared folders, in the next section, we will learn how to create reports and alerts.

Creating reports and alerts

In this section, we will learn how to configure email reports and alerts. QuickSight allows you to configure email reports to update your business users on the latest state of the business.

Email reports are configured against a QuickSight dashboard. To better understand how to set up email reports, we will use the dashboard we created in *Chapter 4, Developing Visuals and Dashboards*. To set up an email report, follow these steps:

1. First, log into Amazon QuickSight as the Author user.

2. Next, open the New York Taxi dashboard.

3. Click the **Share** button, and then select **Email report**, which opens the report configuration screen, as shown in the following figure:

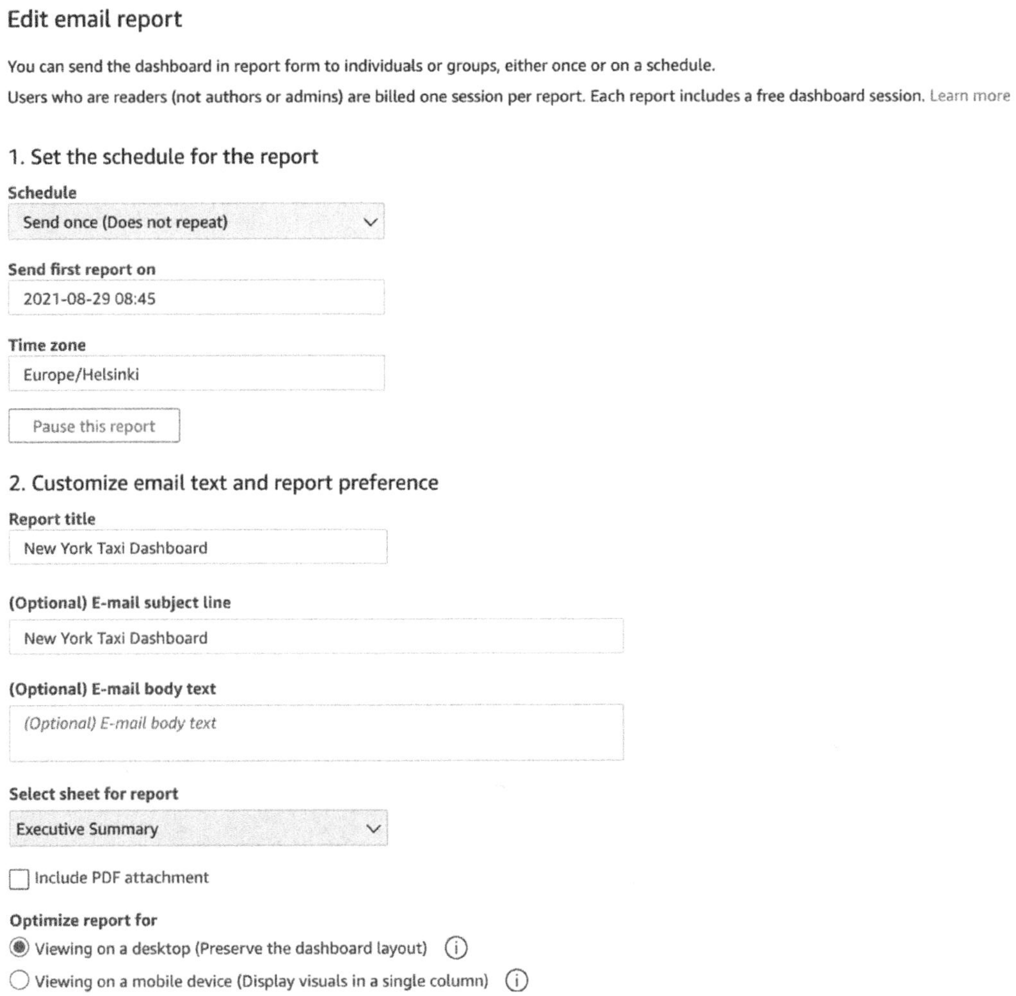

Edit email report

You can send the dashboard in report form to individuals or groups, either once or on a schedule.

Users who are readers (not authors or admins) are billed one session per report. Each report includes a free dashboard session. Learn more

1. Set the schedule for the report

Schedule

| Send once (Does not repeat) | ∨ |

Send first report on

| 2021-08-29 08:45 |

Time zone

| Europe/Helsinki |

| Pause this report |

2. Customize email text and report preference

Report title

| New York Taxi Dashboard |

(Optional) E-mail subject line

| New York Taxi Dashboard |

(Optional) E-mail body text

| (Optional) E-mail body text |

Select sheet for report

| Executive Summary | ∨ |

☐ Include PDF attachment

Optimize report for

◉ Viewing on a desktop (Preserve the dashboard layout) ⓘ

◯ Viewing on a mobile device (Display visuals in a single column) ⓘ

Figure 9.14 – Configuring email reports

4. On the next screen, you can customize your report preferences:

    - **Schedule**: You can set the repeat schedule of your report (send once, repeat once a day, once a week, or once a month) and configure the time when the first report will be sent.

    - **Customize email text and report preferences**: You can customize your report text, including the email title, email text, and report title. You can also select whether the report layout is optimized for mobile screens or desktop screens.

    - **Recipients**: Select the users (these can be either Author or Reader user roles) who will receive the report. You can also choose to email the report to all users with access to this dashboard. If you tick this checkbox, then when you add new users to the dashboard, they will automatically receive the email report.

5. Click **Save report** to complete the email report configuration.

Now that we have configured the email report as the Author user, we will now focus on the Reader user and learn how to manage the report subscriptio:

1. First, log out and log back in as the Reader user.

2. Select **Reports** from the top-right corner menu, as shown in the following screenshot. Note that this option will be visible only when there are email reports configured for this dashboard:

Figure 9.15 – Accessing the report subscription options

3. In the next screen, you can change your report subscription preferences:

    - Choose to subscribe (or unsubscribe) to the report.

    - Choose a desktop/mobile-optimized layout.

These report preferences can be seen in the following screenshot:

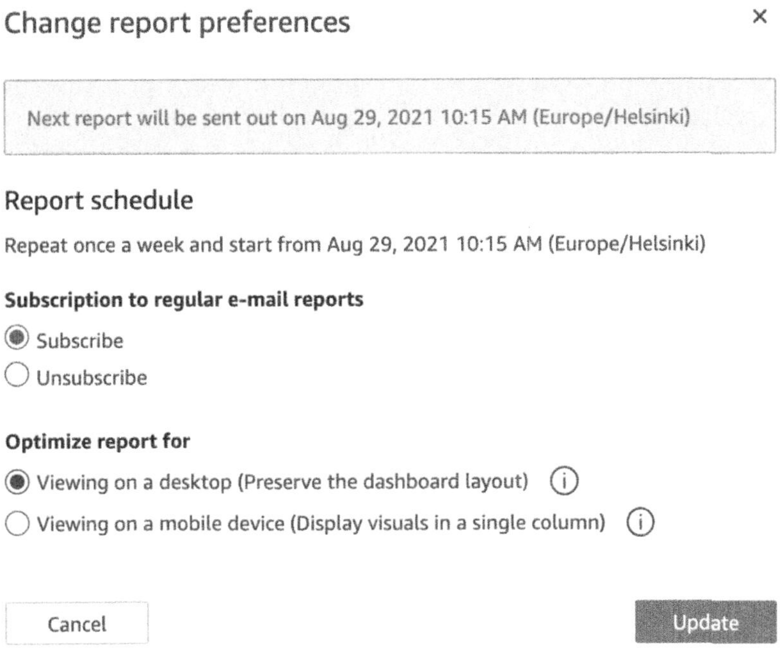

Change report preferences   ✕

Next report will be sent out on Aug 29, 2021 10:15 AM (Europe/Helsinki)

Report schedule

Repeat once a week and start from Aug 29, 2021 10:15 AM (Europe/Helsinki)

Subscription to regular e-mail reports

◉ Subscribe

◯ Unsubscribe

Optimize report for

◉ Viewing on a desktop (Preserve the dashboard layout) ⓘ

◯ Viewing on a mobile device (Display visuals in a single column) ⓘ

Cancel   Update

Figure 9.16 – Managing email report preferences

Now that we have learned how to set up email reports as Authors and how to manage subscriptions as Readers, in the next section, we will learn how to work with QuickSight alerts.

Working with QuickSight threshold-based alerts

QuickSight allows you to set up threshold-based alerts when certain changes occur in your data. Using threshold-based alerts, you can receive notifications when a specific metric changes above or below a certain threshold. For example, when a **key performance indicator** (**KPI**) falls below a target, you get notified so that action can be taken to get the KPI back on target.

> **Note**
> You can have multiple alerts based on different conditions for a specific KPI. Creating different types of alerts for the same metric allows you to implement a complex KPI-monitoring alert system.

In the next section, we will learn how to add threshold-based alerts.

Adding a threshold-based alert

To better understand how to configure threshold-based alerts, we will use the New York Taxi dashboard we developed in *Chapter 4, Developing Visuals and Dashboards*. We will use the *gauge* visual of this dashboard. At the time of writing, there are two visual types that can be configured with alerts:

- **KPI visual**

- **Gauge visual**

To configure threshold-based alerts, complete the following steps:

1. First, log into the QuickSight Console (either as the Author or the Reader user) and open the New York Taxi dashboard.

   > **Note**
   >
   > Threshold-based alerts can only be configured at a QuickSight dashboard, and not on a QuickSight analysis.

2. Next, locate the gauge visual that shows the total number of passengers against a hypothetical target, and click on the visual. Notice the alert (bell) icon on the right-hand side:

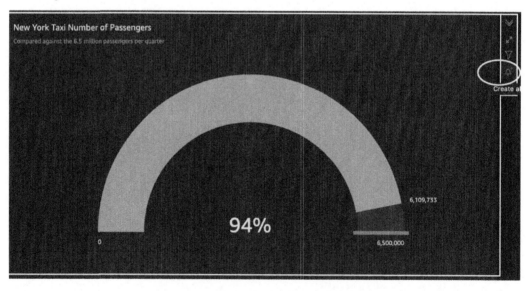

Figure 9.17 – Adding an alert for a gauge visual

3. Click the alert (bell) icon to configure your alert. For this scenario, let's assume we want to add the first alert when our KPI is below the 95% mark of the target. Type the following values:

- **Alert name**: `[Amber] New York Taxi Number of Passengers`

- **Alert value**: `Percent`

- **Condition**: `Is below`

- **Threshold**: `95`

- **Notification preference**: `As frequently as possible`

Alerts for SPICE datasets are evaluated every time the dataset is refreshed. According to the AWS documentation, for direct query datasets, alert rules are evaluated at a random time between 6:00 PM and 8:00 AM in the **AWS Region** that holds the dataset:

`https://docs.aws.amazon.com/quicksight/latest/user/threshold-alerts.html`

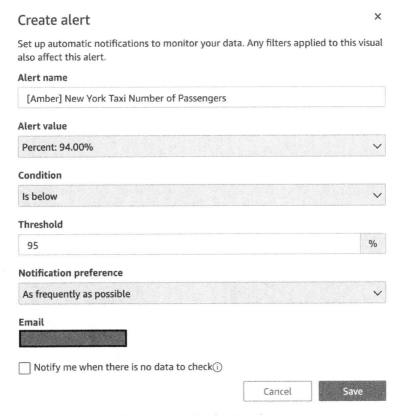

Figure 9.18 – Configuring alerts

4.   Click **Save**. Repeat the process to create a second alert. For the second alert, use the same configuration as the first one, replacing only the `Amber` word with `Red` in the alert name, and set the threshold to `90`.

5.   The next time you refresh your dataset, you will see an example alert in your mailbox, as shown in the following screenshot:

Figure 9.19 – Receiving QuickSight alerts

Now that we have configured two alerts, in the next section, we will learn how to manage alerts.

Managing threshold-based alerts

In this section, we will learn how to manage threshold-based alerts:

1.   Stay logged into the QuickSight Console with the user you used in the previous section. Open the `New York Taxi` dashboard we used in the previous step to set up our alerts.

2.   Click the **Alerts** icon in the top-right corner of your QuickSight dashboard, as shown in the following screenshot:

Figure 9.20 – Accessing the dashboard alerts management console

3. This step will open the alerts management console, as shown in the following screenshot. From this screen, you can view all your dashboard alerts and the conditions that trigger them. You can enable/disable each alert separately by toggling the radio button next to each alert. Finally, you can expand the alert history and view when each alert has been triggered:

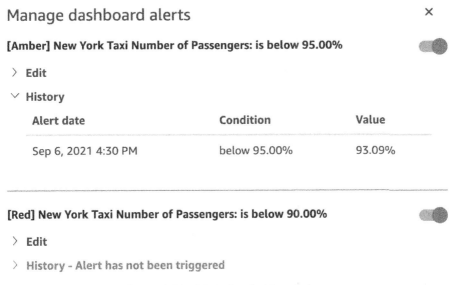

Figure 9.21 – Managing dashboard alerts

4. Using the **Edit** dropdown, you can open each alert and change its name, condition, threshold, and notification preferences. You can also delete the alerts using this option.

By using email reports and threshold-based alerts, you ensure your business users are up to date with your latest dashboards. Your business users will receive email notifications either when new data is available or when certain thresholds are met.

Summary

Congratulations on completing this chapter.

In this chapter, we learned how to configure permissions for our Amazon QuickSight users and groups. We also learned how to define fine-grained permissions, and we discussed the benefits of integrating QuickSight with Amazon Lake Formation. Then, we focused on how best to organize QuickSight assets such as analyses, datasets, and dashboards by using folders, and how to share assets using shared folders. Finally, we learned how to configure automated email reports and how to configure threshold-based alerts.

Using the things you learned in this chapter, you will be able to define your permissions and make sure you manage them effectively, making use of groups and folders where possible.

In the next (and final) chapter, we will learn how to configure and architect multi-tenant QuickSight environments.

Questions

1. What are the benefits of integrating Amazon Lake Formation with QuickSight?

2. What QuickSight visuals support threshold-based alerts?

3. How do we automate email reports?

4. What are the differences between personal and shared folders in Amazon QuickSight, and when should we use them?

Further reading

- *Amazon QuickSight User Guide*:

  https://docs.aws.amazon.com/quicksight/latest/user/amazon-quicksight-user.pdf

10
Multitenancy in Amazon QuickSight

In this chapter, we will learn how to set up multitenancy in **Amazon QuickSight**. Specifically, we will look into multi-tenant architectures and understand how QuickSight namespaces can help us build multi-tenant environments.

We will cover the following topics in this chapter:

- Introducing multitenancy using namespaces
- Setting up multitenancy

Technical requirements

For this chapter, you will need access to the following:

- An **AWS** account and **AWS Identity and Access Management (IAM)** user, with elevated access
- An Amazon QuickSight (Enterprise edition) account with an Admin user configured
- The dashboard created in *Chapter 4, Developing Visuals and Dashboards*

Introducing multitenancy using namespaces

In this section, we will introduce the concept of multitenancy in Amazon QuickSight. Based on what we have learned so far, a user that owns a QuickSight asset can share the resource with any other registered user in the account. However, there are use cases where a single QuickSight account needs to support multiple **tenants**.

Understanding multitenancy

QuickSight offers features that allow developers to build multi-tenant **business intelligence** (**BI**) platforms. Due to its cloud-native architecture, QuickSight scales automatically depending on the number of users. This feature, coupled with QuickSight's embedding capabilities and its API actions that can be accessed programmatically, helps developers to implement multi-tenant BI platforms.

A key characteristic of a multi-tenant platform is that tenants don't interact with each other, which effectively prevents a tenant from granting (or revoking) access to users belonging to another tenant. It is also common that different tenants can have different permission requirements for their users and different *look and feel* requirements. Multi-tenant platforms can serve large corporations, where a tenant can be each subsidiary or a separate department within the company.

Another use case can be software vendors who offer BI capabilities to their customers. In this example, each tenant of the platform would represent a customer of the software vendor. Each tenant would be able to manage their own BI assets and share them with their own users (but not with other tenants). For this scenario, the tenants would typically access QuickSight through a web portal. To separate and organize users from different tenants, QuickSight introduced the concept of *namespaces*.

In the next section, we will introduce QuickSight namespaces.

Introducing QuickSight namespaces

To address multitenancy requirements, Amazon QuickSight introduced the namespace API. The namespace API allows organizations to build multi-tenant environments without the need to create multiple QuickSight accounts.

A QuickSight namespace is a logical container of users and groups, and it can be used to separate different departments or organizations. While users within the same namespace can share assets between themselves, users from different namespaces cannot interact with each other.

A namespace can be one of the following:

- **Default namespace**

- **Custom namespace**

When you create a new QuickSight account, your first Author and Admin users will belong to the *default* namespace. Any other namespaces that you create are *custom* namespaces.

> **Note**
>
> In custom namespaces, only federated SSO users can access the QuickSight console. For other types of users (such as users authenticated with a QuickSight username and password), you should use the default namespace.

A user cannot belong to more than one namespace. It is not possible to move users between namespaces. Other QuickSight assets, such as analysis dashboards and datasets, don't belong exclusively to namespaces. Instead, access to QuickSight assets is managed using the Access API, as we learned in *Chapter 8, Understanding the QuickSight API*. Therefore, it is possible to programmatically share an asset with users from different namespaces. For example, an organization might need to share a common dashboard with all users of all namespaces.

The following figure depicts an example architecture for multi-tenant BI analytics:

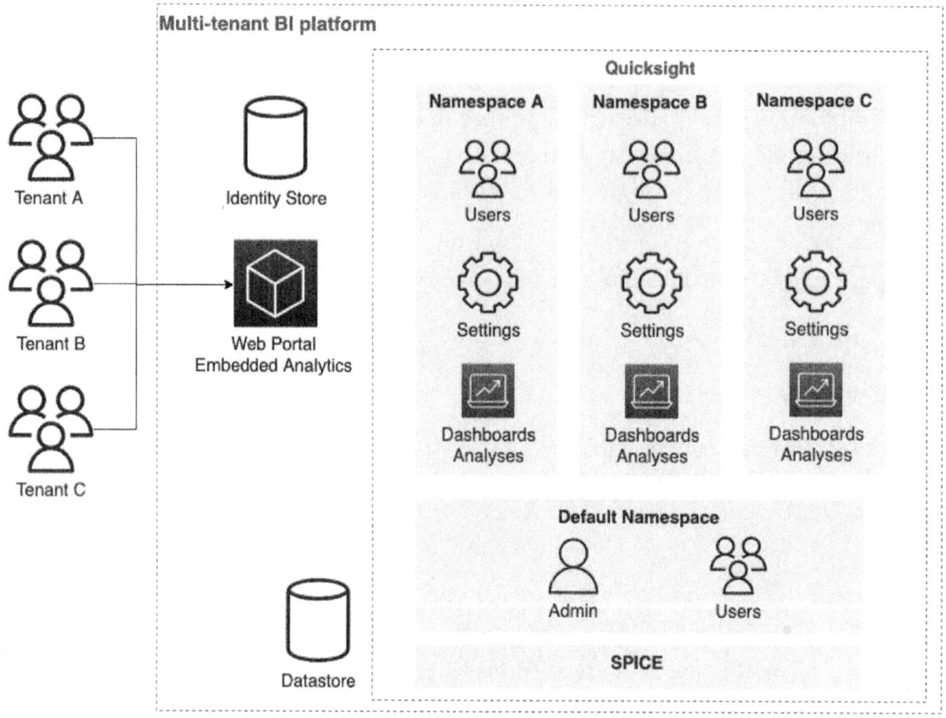

Figure 10.1 – Multi-tenant architecture

The main components of the architecture are as follows:

- **Custom namespaces**: These are to organize the users from different tenants.

- **Default namespace**: These are for Admin users.

- **Amazon SPICE** and **datasets**: These are specific to a QuickSight account. Access to these resources is managed separately using the QuickSight API, as we learned in *Chapter 3, Preparing Data with Amazon QuickSight*, and *Chapter 9, Managing QuickSight Permissions and Usage*.

- **Embedded portal** and **Identity Store**: This allows users into the QuickSight console. For those use cases that don't need an embedded web portal, the QuickSight web app can be used instead. The embedded portal can be any custom-built web app. Implementation details on how to build web applications are outside the scope of this book.

Now that we have learned the fundamentals of using multi-tenant architectures in QuickSight, in the next section, we will look at a hands-on example.

Setting up multitenancy

In this chapter, we will set up a simple multi-tenant environment using the namespace API. This exercise will help you understand how to set up multi-tenant environments as a QuickSight Admin user. It will also help you understand what your BI users' experience will be in multi-tenant scenarios, and how QuickSight prevents users from sharing assets with other tenants.

Creating a namespace

Creating namespaces is simple, and it can be done using the QuickSight API. At the time of writing, it is not possible to create namespaces through the QuickSight **graphical user interface** (**GUI**):

1. First, you need to log into Amazon QuickSight as the QuickSight Admin user.

2. Next, open the **AWS Command Line Interface** (**CLI**), and type the following command, replacing the highlighted values with the values from your environment. For this exercise, we will create a custom namespace called companyA. Note that we already have a default namespace for our existing Admin, Author, and Reader users used throughout this book:

    ```
    $aws quicksight create-namespace --aws-account-id
    <account-id> --namespace companyA --identity-store
    QUICKSIGHT
    ```

    This will result in an asynchronous creation of the new namespace. Note, in the CLI response, the status is CREATING:

    ```
    {
        "Status": 202,
        "Name": "companyA",
        "CapacityRegion": "us-east-1",
        "CreationStatus": "CREATING",
        "IdentityStore": "QUICKSIGHT",
        "RequestId": "xxxxxx-xxxxx-xxxxxxxxxxxxx"
    }
    ```

3. To confirm that the new namespace has been created, we will use the list-namespaces CLI command. Type the following command, replacing the highlighted values with those from your environment:

    ```
    $aws quicksight list-namespaces --aws-account-id
    <aws-account-id>
    ```

Note the response. It should look like the following:

```
{
    "Status": 200,
    "Namespaces": [
        {
            "Name": "companyA",
            "Arn": "arn:aws:quicksight:us-east-
1:<account-id>:namespace/companyA",
            "CapacityRegion": "us-east-1",
            "CreationStatus": "CREATED",
            "IdentityStore": "QUICKSIGHT"
        },
        {
            "Name": "default",
            "Arn": "arn:aws:quicksight:us-east-1:
:<account-id>:namespace/default",
            "CapacityRegion": "us-east-1",
            "CreationStatus": "CREATED",
            "IdentityStore": "QUICKSIGHT"
        }
    ],
    "RequestId": "xxxxxxx-xxx-xxx-xxx-xxx"
}
```

Both namespaces have now been created successfully.

> **Note**
> Namespaces span **AWS Regions**, and a user will be assigned to the same
> QuickSight namespace, regardless of which Region they are using.

Now that we have created our new namespace, in the next section, we will allocate a new
user to the namespace.

Using QuickSight namespaces

In this section, we will add users, and then we will see how namespaces don't allow users
to share assets with other namespaces. At the end of this section, we will learn how we can
configure common assets across namespaces.

Adding users

Now that we have a new namespace, we will register new users using the new namespace. For this exercise, we will register a new IAM user in QuickSight:

1. First, create a new IAM user called `author-a` using the **AWS Console**. Select **IAM**, and then the users from the left-hand side menu.

2. Select **Add users**. On the next screen, choose a user name, and then check the **Password – AWS Management Console access** checkbox, as shown in the following screenshot:

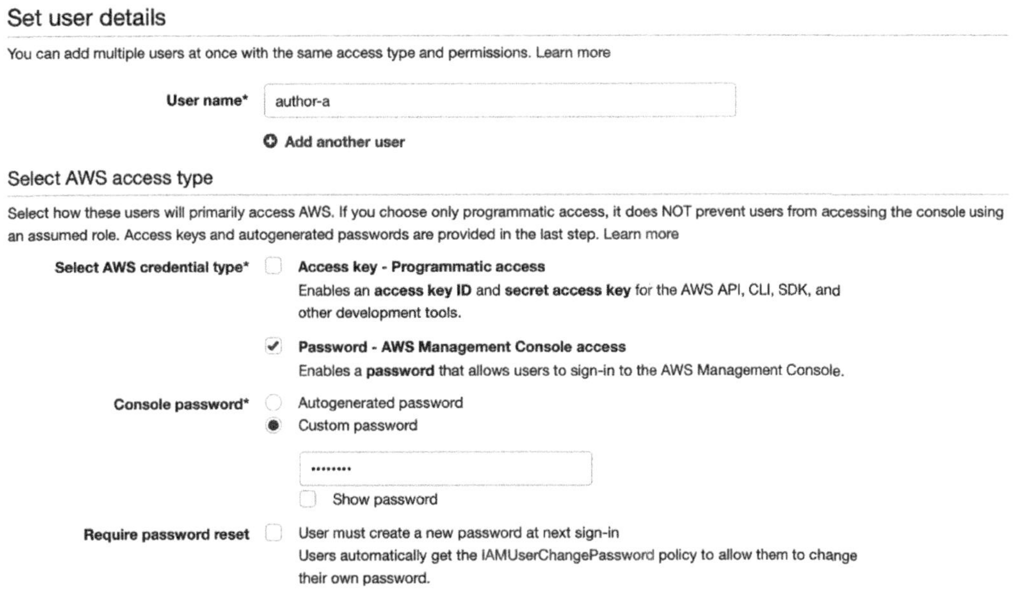

Set user details

You can add multiple users at once with the same access type and permissions. Learn more

| User name* | author-a |

⊕ **Add another user**

Select AWS access type

Select how these users will primarily access AWS. If you choose only programmatic access, it does NOT prevent users from accessing the console using an assumed role. Access keys and autogenerated passwords are provided in the last step. Learn more

Select AWS credential type* ☐ **Access key - Programmatic access**
Enables an **access key ID** and **secret access key** for the AWS API, CLI, SDK, and other development tools.

☑ **Password - AWS Management Console access**
Enables a **password** that allows users to sign-in to the AWS Management Console.

Console password* ○ Autogenerated password
● Custom password

········

☐ Show password

Require password reset ☐ User must create a new password at next sign-in
Users automatically get the IAMUserChangePassword policy to allow them to change their own password.

Figure 10.2 – Creating an IAM user

3. On the next screen, leave the permissions empty and click **Create**. Take note of the user `arn` value, as we will use it in the next step.

4. Now that we have created our new user, we will register them with QuickSight under the `companyA` namespace. Using the CLI, type the following command, replacing the highlighted values with those from your environment:

```
$aws quicksight register-user --identity-type IAM
--email <your-email> --user-role AUTHOR --iam-
arn arn:aws:iam::<aws-account-id>:user/author-a
--aws-account-id <aws-account-id> --namespace companyA
```

To confirm the creation of the user, we will use the `list-users` CLI command. Note that we specify `companyA` as the namespace:

```
$aws quicksight list-users --aws-account-id
<aws-account-id> --namespace companyA
```

The response will look like the following:

```
{
    "Status": 200,
    "UserList": [
        {
            "Arn": "arn:aws:quicksight:us-east-
1:xxxxxxxxxxxx:user/companyA/author-a",
            "UserName": "author-a",
            "Email": "xxx@xxx",
            "Role": "AUTHOR",
            "IdentityType": "IAM",
            "Active": true,
            "PrincipalId": "federated/iam/xxxxx"
        }
    ],
    "RequestId": "xxxx-xxxx-xxxx-xxxx"
}
```

5. Now that we have successfully created our user, let's try to understand the effects of a namespace. Open the AWS Console, and log into QuickSight as the newly created user. Expand the top-right menu. Note the namespace name, as shown in the following screenshot:

Figure 10.3 – Logging in to a multi-tenant QuickSight account

6. Next, we want to ensure that this user cannot share their dashboards, analyses, or datasets with users from other namespaces. The easiest way to check this is to quickly create a new dataset, analysis, or dashboard and try sharing it with other users. Once the asset is created, open its permissions manager and try to invite a Author or Reader user who belongs to a different namespace:

Manage dataset permissions   ✕

You can manage the settings and permissions for users, analyses, and dashboards that access this dataset.

Users	Usage	Q topics

Shared with 1 user

Name	Permission	Actions
🙎 author-a	Owner	

| Close | | Invite users |

Figure 10.4 – Sharing assets in multi-tenant environments

When sharing assets, QuickSight autocompletes when it finds relevant users. You will notice that as you type author, there is no suggestion from QuickSight, and the dataset cannot be shared. The reason for this is that the Author user belongs to a different namespace to the author-a user.

Now that we have seen how namespaces prevent users from sharing assets with other users, we will see how it is possible to configure common assets between users in different namespaces.

Sharing common assets

It is possible to have use cases where assets need to be visible to users that inhabit different namespaces. For example, a large corporation might want to share a specific dashboard with users that belong to different departments, which are configured as namespaces. To complete this action, we will need to use the QuickSight API. As we learned in the previous section, completing this via the QuickSight console is not possible, as users from one namespace cannot discover users from another namespace.

To better understand this concept, we will use the New York Taxi dashboard configured in *Chapter 4*, *Developing Visuals and Dashboards*. For this tutorial, we will use the QuickSight Admin user and the AWS CLI:

1. First, open a terminal with the AWS CLI installed.

2. List the dashboards using the list-dashboard action. Type the following command, replacing the highlighted values with those from your environment:

    ```
    $aws quicksight list-dashboards --aws-account
    <aws-account-id>
    ```

    Focus on the DashboardSummaryList array, and capture the DashboardId value, as we will use it in the next step:

    ```
    "DashboardSummaryList": [
            {
                "Arn": "arn:aws:quicksight:us-east-
    1:xxxxxxxxx:dashboard/xxxx-xxxx-xxxx-xxxx-xxxx",
                "DashboardId": "xxxx-xxxx-xxxx-xxxx-xxxx",
                "Name": "New York Taxi Dashboard",
        ...
            }
    ```

3. To update the dashboard permissions, we will use the update-dashboard-permissions CLI command. Type the following command, replacing the highlighted values with those from your environment:

    ```
    $aws quicksight update-dashboard-permissions --aws-ac-
    count-id <aws-account-id> --dashboard-id <dashboard-id>
    --grant-permissions Actions=quicksight:DescribeDash-
    board,quicksight:ListDashboardVersions,quicksight:Update-
    DashboardPermissions,quicksight:QueryDashboard,quick-
    sight:UpdateDashboard,quicksight:DeleteDashboard,quick-
    sight:DescribeDashboardPermissions,quicksight:UpdateDash-
    boardPublishedVersion,Principal=arn:aws:quicksight:us-
    east-1:<aws-account-id>:user/companyA/author-a
    ```

    Now that we have provided access to our author-a user, we will log in to the QuickSight console and view the available dashboards.

4. Log into the QuickSight console as the author-a user. Then, navigate to **Dashboards** to view the available dashboards. The New York Taxi dashboard should now be available for you to view, as shown in the following screenshot:

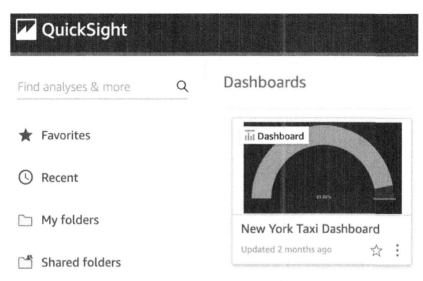

Figure 10.5 – Viewing common assets in a multi-tenant environment

In a similar way to dashboards, other assets (such as datasets or analyses) can be shared using the QuickSight API.

Summary

Congratulations on completing this chapter, which is the final chapter of this book.

In this chapter, we learned about multitenancy in Amazon QuickSight. We also looked closely at an example architecture that allows multiple tenants to access embedded assets in QuickSight through a web portal. Then, we focused on QuickSight namespaces, and we learned how to configure them. Finally, we looked at two hands-on examples to understand how namespaces prevent users from sharing assets, and how an Admin user can configure common assets for users in different namespaces.

You should now understand the fundamental concepts of multitenancy in Amazon QuickSight, and you should know how to use the AWS CLI to create namespaces and organize your different tenants.

Before you close this book, please ensure that all AWS resources created for this book and its exercises are shut down to prevent charges to your AWS account.

I want to thank you for your time, and I hope this book met your expectations. For any comments and further questions, you can find me on LinkedIn. Feel free to connect with me, I would love to hear your thoughts and feedback. Happy learning!

Questions

1. What are the main characteristics of multi-tenant platforms?

2. What are the main use cases for creating multi-tenant BI platforms?

3. What are QuickSight namespaces, and how do you configure them?

Further reading

- *Amazon QuickSight User Guide*: https://docs.aws.amazon.com/quicksight/latest/user/amazon-quicksight-user.pdf

- *Supporting Multitenancy with Isolated Namespaces*: https://docs.aws.amazon.com/quicksight/latest/user/namespaces.html

Packt.com

Subscribe to our online digital library for full access to over 7,000 books and videos, as well as industry leading tools to help you plan your personal development and advance your career. For more information, please visit our website.

Why subscribe?

- Spend less time learning and more time coding with practical eBooks and Videos from over 4,000 industry professionals

- Improve your learning with Skill Plans built especially for you

- Get a free eBook or video every month

- Fully searchable for easy access to vital information

- Copy and paste, print, and bookmark content

Did you know that Packt offers eBook versions of every book published, with PDF and ePub files available? You can upgrade to the eBook version at packt.com and as a print book customer, you are entitled to a discount on the eBook copy. Get in touch with us at customercare@packtpub.com for more details.

At www.packt.com, you can also read a collection of free technical articles, sign up for a range of free newsletters, and receive exclusive discounts and offers on Packt books and eBooks.

Other Books You May Enjoy

If you enjoyed this book, you may be interested in these other books by Packt:

Machine Learning with Amazon SageMaker Cookbook

Joshua Arvin Lat

ISBN: 9781800567030

- Train and deploy NLP, time series forecasting, and computer vision models to solve different business problems Push the limits of customization in SageMaker using custom container images Use AutoML capabilities with SageMaker Autopilot to create high-quality models Work with effective data analysis and preparation techniques Explore solutions for debugging and managing ML experiments and deployments Deal with bias detection and ML explainability requirements using SageMaker Clarify Automate intermediate and complex deployments and workflows using a variety of solutions.

Amazon Redshift Cookbook

Shruti Worlikar, Thiyagarajan Arumugam, Harshida Patel

ISBN: 9781800569683

- Use Amazon Redshift to build petabyte-scale data warehouses that are agile at scale Integrate your data warehousing solution with a data lake using purpose-built features and services on AWS Build end-to-end analytical solutions from data sourcing to consumption with the help of useful recipes Leverage Redshift's comprehensive security capabilities to meet the most demanding business requirements Focus on architectural insights and rationale when using analytical recipes Discover best practices for working with big data to operate a fully managed solution.

Packt is searching for authors like you

If you're interested in becoming an author for Packt, please visit `authors.packtpub.com` and apply today. We have worked with thousands of developers and tech professionals, just like you, to help them share their insight with the global tech community. You can make a general application, apply for a specific hot topic that we are recruiting an author for, or submit your own idea.

Share Your Thoughts

Now you've finished *Actionable Insights with Amazon QuickSight*, we'd love to hear your thoughts! Scan the QR code below to go straight to the Amazon review page for this book and share your feedback or leave a review on the site that you purchased it from.

https://packt.link/r/1-801-07929-3

Your review is important to us and the tech community and will help us make sure we're delivering excellent quality content.

Index

Printed in Great Britain
by Amazon

20477562R00140